CONTENTS

PREFACE

This book consists of 100 tips to help PhD students with their PhDs.

100 Tips are a lot, and trying to implement them all at once can be quite the challenge. Instead, it's much easier to implement a few at a time and once these tips becomes part of your routine, incorporate more. Repeat this process with each of these tips.

To help facilitate this, at the end of the book you will find a summary of these 100 tips for you to quickly reference when needed.

What's more, you may find that certain tips resonate with you more than others. That is completely normal. In fact, as you progress through your PhD, some tips that once resonated so strongly with you will become less important, and others that you didn't find so important will become very valuable to you.

These 100 tips span the range of challenges PhD students face on a daily basis. As such, as per the very helpful suggestion of one of the reviewers of this original manuscript, Geoff Vaughn, each tip has been keyed with an icon just below its title to indicate to the reader whether this tip is a research tip, a well-being tip, a motivation and productivity tip, or a career tip.

A blue star, like the one below, indicates that the tip is a research tip:

A gold star, like the one below, indicates that the tip is a well-being tip:

A red star, like the one below, indicates that the tip is a motivation and productivity tip:

A green star, like the one below, indicates that the tip is a career tip:

Some tips feature more than one colored star because they pertain to more than one type of tip.

Some tips throughout this book relate to each other. Many of them have been spaced apart at different intervals in the book to help remind you of them and to stress their importance.

The development of this book consisted of us here at PhD Voice writing the original manuscript. We wanted to make it as useful as possible so we had 51 people from the PhD Voice community read it and give us feedback on how to improve it. After addressing their constructive feedback, we published this book –

as you see it here.

Thank you to all of these reviewers including, Additi Pandey, Ahmed Ali Jaleel, Aliya Shams, Amy Wallace, Anthony Gifford, Apurva Shyam, Florentine Weber, Geoff Vaughan, Irfan Haider Khan, Juliana Ciccheto, Paulina Montaño, Sarah Ater, Ugochukwu Ezeh, and the 38 others who wished to remain anonymous.

PhD Voice has become a leading figure for PhD students around the world. It has interacted with 100,000s of PhD students, resulting in PhD Voice having unparalleled experience and knowledge of the challenges PhD students face every day.

1. BE YOURSELF, AND NOT SOMEONE ELSE

There are many times throughout your PhD where you may feel the need to pretend or act like someone who isn't really you.

For example, when you first start, to fit in, you might feel the need to pretend like you are someone else.

Another example is when you may not feel good about something, but you pretend that everything is okay, when it isn't. That can come in all shapes and forms, from mentally/emotionally/physically not feeling well, to having doubts about your work, to feeling nervous about presenting your work.

Another example is to agree with someone about some aspect of your work when you don't really agree. Don't be afraid to say what you think because that is what research is all about.

All of these circumstances, and more, can make you want to pretend to be someone other than who you are.

Don't!

The reason is because it leads to unhappiness in the long-run.

If you don't know something, then that's fine. If you don't like something, then that's also fine. If you want to do something, then that is also fine.

Because of how often this feeling pops up, this is the number one tip, and it will appear in may different forms throughout this book. Some of these forms are obvious, like the ones just written, but others are more subtle.

2. PICK A GOOD SUPERVISOR

Arguably the most important component of your PhD is your supervisor. The reason why is because s/he holds so much sway over everything about your PhD, from the topic you will investigate, to what resources you have, to when you will defend, to even getting a job afterward.

The most important quality a supervisor should have is that they have your well-being at heart.

That means that s/he cares about not only how your project is progressing, but also how you are feeling, and about your future.

Kindness is a huge deal, and getting a supervisor who cares about your well-being means that they will inherently be kind.

One great way of determining what a supervisor will be like before you pick, is to see what their former students are doing now and what they have to say. This is very useful because you have hard evidence of what you can expect – these people have had this experience imprint itself on their careers and it is obvious to see now.

In addition to this very useful method, there is so much to talk about when picking a good supervisor, which is why we've written a blog post about it, here: https://phdvoice.org/how-to-pick-a-phd-supervisor/

In this post, we cover may other aspects. Make sure to read it because these few points we mentioned above are the tip of the iceberg.

3. KEEP REGULAR CONTACT WITH YOUR SUPERVISORS

Keeping regular contact with your supervisors is of paramount importance.

Your supervisors, among other things, should have extensive knowledge about your field (especially if you followed tip #2), and even just running things by them means that they will be able to spot potential problems before they happen. This is the best time to spot potential problems because they are the easiest to fix at this stage. The more a problem grows, the harder it is to fix.

Perhaps, you could use a weekly meeting, however, there are times when that may not be practical. Even so, just a weekly email sent to them detailing what you are doing, and just letting them know that you're keeping them in the loop, is effective.

4. BE HONEST WITH YOURSELF AND YOUR SUPERVISORS

Being honest with yourself and your supervisors refers to almost everything about your project. For example, if you're not feeling motivated this week, let them know. Good supervisors (tip #2) understand that you're not going to be 100% motivated 100% of the time. Anyone who thinks this is either inexperienced with supervising or just plain apathetic.

Another example of when you need to be honest is if you have doubts about your research or method. They have additional experience that you can use to help overcome these doubts, whether that means that you have to change something about your method (etc.), or whether that means you need some clarification. Either way, they're there to help.

If your supervisors don't know what trouble you're having, then they can't help you.

The only time when you might not want to be completely open and honest about something is when it is very personal. For example, if you have a death in the family and you don't feel ready to share it with them, then just say that you have an important family issue and need to attend to it.

Just make sure to keep your supervisors in the loop and let them know how you feel about what you're doing.

5. LOVE YOUR PHD TOPIC

The PhD road is long, which is why loving your topic is very important. It will give you motivation when you need it.

What's more, you will also do better research on a topic you love than a topic you don't. The is because when we truly love an activity, we put far more effort and thought into it. We become less distracted when doing it and the work we do put into it doesn't really feel like work.

As a result, this will make your PhD much stronger.

That will make it easier getting a job afterward, but it will also increase how much you develop during your PhD.

A PhD, at its core, is not really about publishing papers or even setting you up to get a good job afterward, these are just by-products.

At its core, a PhD is about improving you. Lean into that philosophy and you will reap greater rewards from your PhD than a simple piece of paper at the end.

Pick a topic that you love.

6. HAVE THE RIGHT EXPECTATIONS, NOT NECESSARILY "REALISTIC"

Avery common problem many PhD students encounter is that the question that they choose for their PhDs is actually a rabbit hole – it becomes so complex and far broader than first thought.

This is normal for an inexperienced researcher and something that a PhD teaches you – after learning about this, you become much better at honing a research question.

Assuming that the PhD student is diligent, this rabbit hole arises for two main reasons. The first is that the initial question seemed narrow enough to "realistically" answer during the PhD. The second reason is that the supervisors didn't point out the broadness of the question.

For the second reason, you can mitigate this by choosing good supervisors to begin with (tip #2) AND by asking them about the question – ask them if it's too broad, or if they think you can answer it with the few years you have in your PhD.

For the first reason, not gaging the "realistic-ness" of your question given the PhD constraints, a good rule of thumb is to make the question narrower than you think you should.

Even if you think that the question is already too narrow, make it a little narrower because you are also guaranteed to find out in the coming years, and even months, that the question is already far broader than you first realized.

Make your question a little narrower.

7. FORMULATE THE "QUESTION" OF YOUR PHD SIMPLY

If you can't simply explain what your PhD is about, then you don't truly understand it.

That's a motto that many researchers have benefited by using.

The major reason why this is so important is because the better you understand the focus of your PhD, the more readily you can identify whether methods, information, and even journals fit your project.

In short, your PhD will be more focused, which is exactly what your PhD should be.

So, try to formulate your PhD's focus so that a 5 year old can understand it. Once you get to that stage, you'll know that you truly understand what your PhD is about.

8. WHEN FIRST STARTING, SEE YOUR LIBRARIANS

Librarians are a phenomenal resource AND they're greatly under-utilized by researchers in general.

Librarians can help your PhD by helping you find relevant journals for your topic. They can also teach you how to search on the internet for information about your topic more effectively.

Librarians also help you get copies of books and papers that you wouldn't have access to otherwise. All you need to do is see them, ask them if they can get hold of it, and let them do their magic.

As I said, they're an incredible resource, whose helpfulness is only overshadowed by how little people realize it.

In addition to using them at the start of your PhD, feel free to keep going back throughout your PhD and research career.

9. TAKE ADVANTAGE OF RESOURCES AVAILABLE AT YOUR LIBRARY

In tip #8, we instructed to make use of your librarian because s/he is incredibly knowledgeable and will help you greatly.

Similarly, take advantage of the resources your library has to offer. You might be thinking that you didn't even know that the library has anything to offer, other than books and papers.

If you are thinking that, then you must pay a visit to your library, or check them online.

Their resources often range from classes and courses on writing, to laptops you can borrow, to workspaces and meeting rooms to book (with Zoom/Skype capabilities), to even just a desk with a nice view.

You'll almost always find something useful at your library.

10. MAKE A PLAN OF YOUR PHD

One of the most useful things you can do is to make a plan of your PhD project.

Initially, this plan will be fairly generic with few details, and that's completely normal. As you start understanding what your PhD will entail, the plan will become more detailed.

The major benefit of a plan is not that it will keep your project on schedule – ideally it will, but even if it doesn't, by making a plan, you'll gain something even more important – clarity.

If you're like everyone else, it's hard to keep dozens of different items in your head and juggle them around, especially if they are time-related. That's where having a plan helps. By putting down the various tasks you need to do, you can readily identify bottlenecks and potential hold-ups to your work.

Many tasks can be done in parallel and don't rely too heavily on each other. But, some tasks must be done in series and greatly rely on other tasks and factors. Making a plan highlights these bottlenecks and helps you resolve the potential problems before they arise.

Sure, it would be great if the plan's timeline came true, but even if it doesn't, you will still have gained valuable insight into your project by doing one.

One common way of making a plan is to make a "Gantt Chart". Most spreadsheet softwares, like Excel, Google Sheets, and LibreOffice Calc, have the ability to do this. Here is a 7-minute video on YouTube thoroughly showing this functionality in Excel: https://www.youtube.com/watch?v=ByimCyYnl2Y.

This is what a typical Gantt Chart looks like – there are tasks on the left with the start and end dates, and a visual representation of them on the right:

11. KEEP AN UP-TO-DATE PLAN OF YOUR WORK

Following on from tip #10, in addition to making a plan, make sure to keep it up-to-date. It's easy to make a plan at the start of your PhD and then leave it for two or three years.

By keeping it up-to-date, you keep reminding yourself of what needs to be done next, as well as understand how the workload for your PhD may be changing. It also helps you identify tasks that aren't actually adding anything to your PhD but are just sucking up your time. You can cut those tasks out only if you can identify them. A plan does that.

So, make sure to set aside 15 or 20 minutes every week to go over your plan. You may not like having to spend that much time on it, but over time, that small investment will pay off big.

When should you go over your plan?

The answer to this is fairly personal. For example, I, personally, like doing this on a Friday afternoon for a couple of reasons.

The first is that it's a nice end to the week to help me see what I've done and what lays ahead.

The second reason is that on Friday afternoons, I'm usually a little tired and doing an easy task like this is very doable and I'm still staying productive.

Another popular time to go over your plan and keep it up-to-date is first thing on Monday. Some people like this approach because it helps them get ready for the week.

Whatever time works for you, do that. But, <u>just make sure you do it!</u>

12. WORK SMARTER, NOT HARDER

Have you even been so determined to do a task that even taking five minutes off to think about improving the way of doing it is out of the question? I know I have, and it's a feeling I need to suppress routinely otherwise I will never find a more efficient way of doing a task.

Getting more work done is not really about working harder. It's about working smarter. There are only so many hours in a day and once you've used them all up, the only way to increase your work output is through making your processes more efficient.

What's more, to make your life less stressful, you need to reduce the number of hours you work. The only way of doing that is through finding a more efficient way of doing your tasks.

Like in tip #11, you may loathe taking time out to do something "that isn't really producing anything", but it's vital and in reality, it actually is producing something.

The time you invest will, sooner or later, pay off big when you find a much better way of doing something and you'll save A LOT more time.

How do you figure out how to do something smarter?

One of the easiest ways is simply to search it the internet. So much of what we do can be automated, and much of the stuff that can't be automated can be simplified and someone has already figured out how to do it.

Alternatively, you can look at what is taking up your time, then see why it is taking so long – identify the bottlenecks and see how to speed them up.

For example, say you want to get all the abstracts of a bunch of papers from a website. Instead of manually going through and copying and pasting, you could write a Python code that does it. If you don't know Python (the programming language), or even any programming language, then this can seem like a daunting task. And it might not be worth doing. BUT, you can always look for software that does this for you – this type of software is called, "web scraping", and other people have already figured out how to do it easily.

13. FIND AND APPLY FOR RESEARCH GRANTS AND SCHOLARSHIPS

One of the biggest problems for PhD students is lack of income.

Some PhD students are fortunate enough to have good stipends, but many are not.

It's no secret that having a larger stipend helps make your life easier and less stressful.

Interestingly, there are many scholarships and grants available for PhD students. Most of them aren't very well-known.

Let me give you an example. When I was doing my PhD, a friend in another department knew of a scholarship that department was giving. It was $5,000.

He applied for it...and got it!

How?

Because he was the only one who applied for it.

Some types of scholarships and grants often available include, for people from low-income situations, for travel, for conferences, for books, for lab materials, for workshops and courses, for public relations. Yes, you read that last one right – some universities and departments will actually give you money so they can use your face/image in some of their advertising.

How can you find these funds?

Trawl through your department's and university's webpages, ask the administrative staff in your department, ask your supervisors, and even ask other PhD students.

14. READ UP ON EVERYTHING YOU CAN ABOUT YOUR TOPIC BEFORE YOU START YOUR DISSERTATION

Being knowledgeable about your topic before you start your dissertation is obviously very beneficial because you'll know what you're doing.

However, it's also important from the point of view that you want to make sure that you're not doing something someone else has already done.

You definitely don't want to start on a topic that has already been done because that is not the point of research.

What's more, you don't want to get years into your PhD only to learn that what you're doing has already been done.

So, make sure to read extensively so you can pick a unique topic.

You can always use that web scraping approach mentioned in tip #13 for abstracts to help you skim a bunch of papers quicker.

15. MAKE NOTES OF EACH PAPER YOU'VE READ IN A SIMPLE SPREADSHEET

There will be A LOT of reading during your PhD. You might read anywhere between 100 and 1,000 papers throughout the entire process. What's more, much of this reading is done when you first start.

Imagine trying to remember what the salient points of a paper were a couple of years after you read it!

You might be able to do that with the few very relevant papers to your topic, but the other hundred papers that you read will be largely forgotten about.

That's why making a simple spreadsheet with summaries of each paper you've read is hugely helpful.

The spreadsheet doesn't need to be fancy, in fact, we have a simple template for you to use on our website. You can download it for free here: https://phdvoice.org/free-resources/

You might be tempted to skip filling in this spreadsheet. Don't. A few minutes spent now doing it will save you hours upon hours of reading in a few years' time, or even a few months' time. That's a pretty good trade-off, isn't it?

16. DON'T BE INTIMIDATED BY THE PROCESS OF GOING TO GRADUATE SCHOOL

When you first think of grad school, you might be inclined to think that everyone there is so SMART. They are all far smarter than you and have far more experience. What business do you have being there??

This is a perfectly natural thought, but it's wrong, and I mean that in the nicest possible way.

First of all, even if it's true that they are smarter than you (which they are likely not), intelligence is not the only factor determining whether you're right for the PhD process.

In fact, I'd go so far as to say that the intelligence you have at the start of your PhD isn't that important at all.

This is because no one who hasn't done a PhD knows what it takes to do a PhD, yet.

So, it doesn't matter how intelligent someone is, they are not more suited to doing a PhD than anyone else.

A PhD is all about taking someone of a certain level and training them to be able to do research effectively. If you got into grad school, then you fit the bill.

If you already had the skills required to get a PhD, then there'd be no reason for you to do a PhD – it would be a waste of your time.

So, don't get intimidated by grad school or other people there who may seem like they know a lot more than you.

If they do, that's fine, but that doesn't mean that you're at a disadvantage because you have already met the requirements to do a PhD.

Finally, most people think other people are smarter than them because everyone is comparing their "behind the scenes" reel with everyone else's "highlight" reel. We only see the highlights of other people, not what's going on in their heads. So, naturally, we will discredit our own abilities.

17. DON'T WORRY ABOUT GETTING EVERYTHING DONE

It's very common to feel overwhelmed by the amount of work you have to do.

When you first start, you're staring at this project that will take years. And even toward the end when you're writing your dissertation, you still have this 300 page *thing* to write!

It is easy to feel overwhelmed by all of this work. But, the most effective way of overcoming and subduing this feeling is to follow tips #10 and #11 – make a plan of your PhD and update it regularly.

Once you've done that, pick the very next task that needs to be done and forget about your plan until the next scheduled time for updating it.

Just take one step at a time and focus ONLY on that immediate task.

Trust in your plan because once you've made the plan as good as you can, further worry is not helpful. Further worry achieves nothing. Just focus on that next task, and only that next task. Just take that next step. Then the next one. Then the next one.

And keep going like that.

18. IF A PROJECT SEEMS LIKE TOO MUCH WORK, BREAK IT DOWN INTO SMALLER STEPS

And following on from tip #17 (and tips #10 and #11), if you ever feel overwhelmed, break whatever you're doing into smaller tasks.

For example, one of the most common "welcome to the jungle" moments new PhD students have, is when they first arrive, they immediately have to do a literature review of their field.

Literature reviews are very large tasks that take months to do, and sometimes even longer.

Saying to yourself, "The next task is to do my literature review", is good in that you've identified what needs to be done, but it is a very large, overarching task, that consists of many smaller tasks.

Simply thinking that the next task is to do your literature review can be demotivating because of how much work there is.

Instead, you could say to yourself, "The next task is to read <u>this</u> paper".

Or, "The next task is to update my Excel spreadsheet with notes about <u>this</u> paper" (tip #15).

Each one of these tasks is manageable, and hence, suitable to be the next task to focus on.

19. WORK ON AT LEAST TWO THINGS AND ALTERNATE BETWEEN THEM

Many people who know me remark how I'm always focused and motivated. One of my secrets is to work on at least two projects and alternative between them.

It's quite an ingenious tip I stumbled upon.

Why would you want to work on more than one thing at a time?

The reason why is because it helps keep you motivated.

To understand this, let's ask ourselves, "Why do we get demotivated?"

We get demotivated because we no longer feel like we are achieving our goal.

Think about times in your life when you felt like you were achieving your goal. Were you motivated then? I bet you were, as I always have been too.

When we have a little win, we feel like a million bucks and want to keep going.

On the other hand, when do we feel demotivated?

Think about a time when you tried and tried but were met with failure. During this time, did you feel motivated to keep going? Probably not.

This is because you saw that your effort had no positive effect – it didn't help you reach your goal...so why try? The reason why we get demotivated is actually very logical and if you ever feel demotivated, then there's nothing wrong with you, there's actually everything right with you, because only an idiot would feel motivated if they continually saw all of their efforts go to waste.

How does working on two or more projects help?

Well, have you ever left a project that you felt demotivated about (even hated), only to return at a later date and feel much better about it? Or, even have some great new ideas on how to approach the problem you have? Yes, everyone has had these experiences. It's completely normal.

That's where having two or more projects helps; whenever you feel like you've hit a wall on one project, switch to the other project.

The exercise of simply getting away from the troublesome project is greatly beneficial. Then when you return to this troublesome project, you will have some new fervor to continue.

I know what you're thinking, "But what if both of my projects are giving me trouble?"

This question always comes up whenever I share this little secret with people.

The answer is very simple – it doesn't matter.

Just the very act of switching to another project for a few hours gives you the impression that you're being productive, which helps you stay motivated.

That little extra motivation helps you stick with the problem a little bit longer. Over time, and several switches later, you will solve the problem.

20. DON'T FORGET ABOUT YOURSELF AS WELL!

One of the easiest ways to forget about your work and get away for a while is to take time off to do something completely unrelated.

This is something that so many PhD students struggle with, especially as they near the end. The trap that's so easy to fall into is the thought pattern that if you're not working right now, then you're not moving forward with your PhD.

That may seem like the case, on the face of it. But, this thought pattern is actually very flawed.

The reason why this thought pattern is so easy to adopt is because we humans are physical creatures. If we don't see something happening, then we assume that nothing is happening.

On the contrary, much of the development you go through during your PhD occurs when you're not even doing your PhD.

To demonstrate this, let me ask you if you've ever had the sensation of leaving a problem, only to come back to it days or even months later and suddenly know how to solve it?

How is that possible? Apparently, we weren't working on it when we were taking time away from it, but somehow we now know how to do it.

Something obviously happened in that time we took off. If nothing happened, then how can we now understand how to solve it?

That time off gives your subconscious mind time to figure things out for you.

What's more, that time off allowed us to relax and when we relax, our minds are no longer in a fight-or-flight state. That fight-or-flight state, which results from stress, means that our creativity drops because all we focus on is what we already know in order to overcome our current obstacle.

When we relax, our minds become more creative because we're not focused on survival (see tip #93).

You may think that it's a little extreme to think that we're in such a stressed state that we're literally feeling like our well-being is threatened...but is it so extreme to think?

Have you ever cried because something in your research didn't work out? Have you ever been so worried about something that EVERYTHING takes a backseat to it?

It's normal to be emotionally invested in your PhD. That emotional tie comes with a lot of stress.

The only way to recover from the detrimental effects, both health-wise and productivity-wise, is to take time away.

One good rule is to make sure you take 30 minutes off every day just to do whatever you like. It could be playing with your dog – or your neighbor's dog. It could literally be doing nothing, if you want. Just schedule it into your daily routine.

One important note; these 30 minutes are not for, "I'll go to the supermarket to get food" because that is also a task you must do. This task is not a break from everything – it's still a burden. These 30 minutes are for doing something random that you like doing and not for filling with other errands.

21. SET ASIDE TIME EVERY DAY TO REFLECT

Following on from tip #20, make sure to also reflect on your PhD, and even your life and well-being, every day.

When was the last time you thought about how your PhD was going? When was the last time you thought about how you were feeling, both physically and emotionally?

Use this time to reflect about how your day went, as well. What went well, what went poorly.

This helps keep things in perspective so that when things go wrong or someone criticizes something about your work, you'll be able to see how far you've come in such a short amount of time!

22. DO THE WORK, BUT DON'T STRESS OVER IT

Once you have your plan and you know what needs to be done today, go about doing it.

What's more, a very simple, yet trying, trick is to not stress over getting everything done that you have planned. Simply put, methodically go about doing what you planned.

If you don't happen to get everything done today, then that's fine. There is always tomorrow.

And don't stress about doing a task or not getting everything done you wanted to, because that can lead to procrastination in the long-run. The way this cycle works is that you initially stress that you haven't done everything, then you work harder. Then you run out of time to do other things you enjoy (tip #20).

Over time, you feel like you don't have a life and that you don't enjoy your life any more. As a result, you aren't motivated to do your PhD work and you just sit there procrastinating to get away from it. Then, you feel guilty for not having done anything on your PhD, so you work longer and later, and this cycle amplifies.

To stop this cycle from happening, don't stress over not getting everything done.

23. DON'T WORRY ABOUT YOUR DISSERTATION

Don't worry about your dissertation. This shouldn't be interpreted as, "don't do your dissertation", but as in, "don't stress about your dissertation".

Like in tip #20, stressing affects our productivity. The more you stress, the less effective you become in the long-run for a variety of reasons. One reason is that you become fatigued. Another reason is that you become annoyed that your life just revolves around the same thing and you never get to enjoy yourself. Another reason is that your mental health plummets. All of these reasons are valid enough to avoid stressing.

However, writing your dissertation is naturally stressful, that's completely normal. And that's why it is challenging to not stress out about it.

What are some approaches to avoid stressing?

One of the first ways is to pick good supervisors (tip #2). Picking good supervisors comes with a whole array of benefits, including the emotional support from them, which helps you feel like you know what you're doing.

Another way to avoid stressing about your dissertation is to set small goals (tip #18) – a dissertation is a massive task. Have you ever written 80,000 words before? It's really, really hard. It's easy to get demoralized if you goal is, "Write 80,000 words". You can't do that in one day, or even one week. For most people, it takes several months of hard work. That's a long time to go without a pat on the back. Instead, set goals for each month, week, day, and even hour if you need. For example, "I need to get 300 words written about this method before I have lunch in 3 hours". For this goal, you have specified what you need to get done and given yourself a time limit (tip #26) to help you achieve your goal.

If you don't achieve your goal, then that is obviously deflating, but instead of becoming dejected, use that emotion to look at why you didn't achieve it. Was there something about the task that made it unachievable? It happens! We often set goals that are far too unrealistic without even knowing it.

Analyze why you didn't achieve the goal, then use your findings to help you set more achievable goals in the future.

For example, right now, I'm writing this tip. I know from experience that I need a break before writing the next tip (tips #25), so instead of trying to just power through, I'm going to take a break. Powering through might work this time, but if I keep doing it, then I will wear out and even a simple goal of writing one tip in this sitting will become insurmountable.

So, without further ado. I will take a break before writing the next tip (tip #99).

24. IT'S OKAY TO BE A LITTLE LAZY SOMETIMES!

It's definitely okay to be lazy sometimes. Feeling lazy is just our way of getting away from something we don't want to do. Sometimes, we don't fulfil tips #22 and #23.

In other words, the stress has caused us to be unmotivated.

Getting re-motivated cannot be done sustainably through willpower. The more you push through something you don't like, the more you'll resent it. The more you resent it, the more willpower you need.

Sooner or later, the amount of willpower you need to overcome that thing you dread will be more than you have.

Instead, being a little lazy now is fine because that's our way of enjoying ourselves. It's our way of telling ourselves that we've had enough of that thing we currently resent and we need a break.

Taking breaks is good for morale.

25. WORK IN SHORT BURSTS

Working in short bursts is ideal for keeping up motivation.

We work most efficiently when we work in short bursts.

The more efficient you are, the less time you need to do a task.

The less time you need, the more time you have to do other things you enjoy, as well.

What's more, the less time you spend on a task, the more you'll like it.

It's far better to do 15 minutes of highly focused work and take a 45 minute break, then work for the full 60 minutes. This is because it's almost impossible to stay focused for 60 minutes straight.

If you doubt this, the next time you're in a lecture, look around periodically to see how many people keep focus for the full 60 minutes.

One very useful technique for working in short bursts is something called, "The Pomodoro Technique". This is where you set a certain amount of time on a clock, perhaps 15 minutes, and work for that time. When the bell chimes, you get to take a break, including checking your phone or emails – but not before! Work for those 15 minutes.

The word, "pomodoro" means, "tomato" in Italian, which I wish I didn't know because it makes me hungry every time I think about it. But, if you can overcome that, then this technique is both fun and effective.

Focus on doing short, highly focused work instead of marathon sessions of work.

26. SET TIME LIMITS FOR YOURSELF

Acorollary to the last tip is to set time limits for how long you will work on something.

This is related to Parkinson's law: The more time you allot something, the more time it will take to complete. So, by reducing that time you've allotted, you work more efficiently.

Now, remember to also take breaks and work in short bursts (tips #25 and #99) because you can't work at a very high efficiency for very long.

By approaching your work this way, you will have more time to screw around and enjoy yourself. That is key for keeping up morale and motivation. The more drawn out something becomes, the more of a "motivation suck" it becomes.

27. MANAGE YOUR TIME EFFECTIVELY

Arguably, the major cause of stress during a PhD is poor time management.

Time management is not just about allocating the right amount of time to a task (see tip #26), it's also about understanding what tasks deserve any time at all.

Some things don't deserve any of our time, and even the few seconds we spend thinking about whether they deserve any of our time or not is just a waste!

Through proper planning (tips #10 and #11), correct allotment of time (tip #26), and accurately identifying what actually deserves time to begin with, you can get on top of your daily tasks.

When I tell people (and not just PhD students, but people in general) this, they then often say that they are doing this but they still aren't on top of their daily tasks. In this case, they are not allotting the correct amount of time to each task, selecting too many tasks to do in a single day, and/or choosing to do tasks that shouldn't be done.

They then say that they don't get to choose what tasks need to be done, but someone else (like their supervisor) assigns them.

In this situation, you still have complete control because you just have to let your supervisor in on the secret that there is only so much time. Working longer hours results in a drop in efficiency and a drop in productivity over time.

These are facts. If you say this dispassionately, then you will sooner or later convince them. The trick is not to get emotional – have you ever noticed how when someone says something in a dispassionate, yet matter-of-fact way, people believe him/her? On the other hand, if the person says the exact same thing, but in an emotional way, some doubt still remains.

It may take several times to reiterate the fact presented above, but done each time, dispassionately, will result in your supervisor getting it through his/her head.

This will force her/him to get better at project management as well, as s/he will be forced to make better plans and identify what needs to be done and when, and what can be done!

Another problem that arises is figuring out what what is an effective use of your time?

To answer this, ask yourself: "If I could only do one thing today, what would it be?"

This task is determined by your plan (tip #10).

Once you have identified that task, do it. When you've done that task, iterate through this process until you've finished for the day or reached your scheduled break time (tip #99).

28. BE FLEXIBLE

It is quite normal for things not to go as planned during your PhD (remember in tip #10). Having a plan is great for getting the different tasks ordered, but sometimes the timing doesn't work out, or even the initial details were too broad.

The major difference between those who thrive in their PhDs and those who don't are whether they can "roll with the punches" or not.

Maybe one day you'll enter the lab and some equipment you were going to use is missing. That puts you behind in your plan because you won't be able to get back into the lab for another month. Maybe there will be a global virus that results in countries being shutdown for months on end. That wasn't in the plan, yet it still can happen!

Regardless of the setback, being flexible and seeing how you can still move forward is what will determine whether you thrive or not.

Just keep rolling with the punches, always looking for how you can use the current situation to your advantage.

29. INVEST IN SOME GOOD STATIONARY SUPPLIES, LIKE PENCILS AND PENS

Following on from tips #27 and #28, good stationary make a big difference to your PhD.

One reason is that having the items you need to do your work is obviously vitally important. What's more, having them right where you need them, is also important. Some estimates say that the average person wastes about 20% of their day just shuffling items around on their desk while trying to find the right thing, and going looking for a piece of stationary that they need.

20% is a big number. That's about 1.5 hours per day. Imagine what you could do with that additional 1.5 hours per day. You could leave 1.5 hours early and even watch a whole movie!

Having the items you need, and organized so you can find them, is a game-changer.

Another reason why having the right stationary is important is because good stationary is ergonomical. For example, did you know that you can get computer mouses/mice that are much more ergonomical than the standard type? Some brands aren't any more expensive, either.

Having an ergonomical mouse reduces the strain on your hand, which makes your life more pleasant, and the time spent on your PhD more productive.

The same thing applies to many other stationary items. For example, you can get pens that are more comfortable than others. You can get shelving that you can organize your papers in so you have more space on your desk. That way, you can place your computer, current paper, and any other items you need, in an ergonomical setup.

When you're getting your stationary, just look for the more ergonomical versions.

30. TEACH YOUR SUBJECT!

The best way to learn is to teach others.

Teaching others is so beneficial for a number of reasons.

The first reason is that you have to clearly understand the thoughts in your head before you can even try to communicate them effectively. Teaching forces you to do that.

The second reason is that before we teach, we often don't realize how many gaps in our knowledge there are. But, when we are preparing to teach, we then start thinking about all of the questions we might be asked, and then we start thinking of the answers. This process helps you learn your subject inside-out.

The third reason is that teaching forces us to communicate effectively. We have to determine which words to use to convey the meanings we want. We also have to determine which words not to use because they may convey different connotations. What's more, we may think of analogies or examples to help others understand a principle.

If you have the opportunity to teach, take it, especially if you're getting paid for it. If you're not getting paid for it, then I recommend doing it only once or twice to get familiar with teaching, but after that, you can decide whether the trade-off is worth it.

If you never get the opportunity to teach, then there is a very useful method to simulate it. Get a yellow, rubber duck and explain your research to it.

This is a very revered method in some fields.

The reason why this is such an effective tool is because it is a kids' toy, and as such we immediately start simplifying what we're saying to match the level of expertise we naturally associate with this duck! The simpler you can explain your research, the better you understand it.

31. GET TEACHING EXPERIENCE

In tip #30, we said to teach your subject because it will greatly help you improve your understanding of it.

But that's not all you will gain from teaching.

Teaching any subject, not just your own, or even just hosting an information day at your university (especially if it is paid), will help you improve your communication skills.

It will also help you overcome any fears or reservations you have about standing in front of a group of people.

It will also help improve your charisma. Trying to get 100 students to focus on you can be challenging. People with higher levels of charisma make it look easy, and that's because it is easy for them. But, almost everyone who is very good at keeping people focused on them, at some point in their lives, sucked at it. They got better through practice.

32. JOIN PUBLIC SPEAKING CLASSES, LIKE TOASTMASTERS

One very effective way of improving your communication skills is by taking public speaking classes.

One of the best is Toastmasters. They have branches in most major cities in the West. They are also very affordable with annual membership being around $100 (depending on where you live). They have meetings every week.

If you want to see how effective you can become at communicating, simply go to the Toastmaster's website and look at the message from the president (https://www.toastmasters.org/leadership-central/message-from-the-international-president). Notice how eloquent he is, his word choice, and how his tonality changes with what he is saying to give the meaning he wants to convey. He is a very effective public speaker.

Better public speaking skills will serve you well in everything you do because everything we do, whether directly or indirectly, involves communication with other people. The better you can do this, the more you will gain. For example, would communicating more effectively during your dissertation defense benefit you?

Yes.

33. WRITE EVERY DAY

One of the most important skills you develop during your PhD is the ability to communicate. Like public speaking, writing is a form of communication.

The better you write, the more succinct and impactful your papers and dissertation will be. What's more, the less hassle it will be to get them accepted.

That's why writing every day (or at least, trying to write every day) is important. The more you write, the better you get at it.

One common idea is that if you write each day, then by the end of your PhD, your dissertation will be written without you having to set aside time to write huge chunks. This is not quite true because you can't really write much of your dissertation at the start of your PhD – you don't know what to write. What's more, by the end of your PhD, you will think about your project very differently to when you started. Things will be much clearer and some ideas you had at the start of your PhD will seem ridiculous and nonsensical – it's normal. Even today, I look back at my earlier ideas and think, "these were good efforts, but severely lacking in understanding".

However, writing each day helps us clarify our ideas and over time, our understanding of our projects becomes much better.

So, even if you write just 100 words per day about what you're doing, it will greatly improve your skills, which will help you write your dissertation at the end, too.

34. DON'T BE AFRAID TO ASK FOR HELP WHEN YOU NEED IT!

Your PhD is not solely done by you.

If you look at any dissertation, you will find the acknowledgements section. That contains a list of different people who helped this person do his/her PhD.

Asking for help is not a sign of weakness. In fact, it's usually a sign of strength. This is because a strong person is capable of being honest with her/himself. A weak person is not. A weak person will deny needed help when s/he needs it whereas a strong person will not.

Your PhD is important to you. If you need help, then getting help will move you farther along the path. It is only sensible to ask for help.

The first time asking for help is the scariest, but once you do, you'll realize that people won't think any less of you. In fact, it will likely strengthen the bonds between you.

Each subsequent time you ask for help becomes easier.

35. YOU'LL GET USED TO DEALING WITH STRESS

Many of the tips given in this book, such as tips #19, #20, #21, #22, #23, and #24 are there to reduce the stress you feel during your PhD.

The fact is that all of these tips reduce the stress, but none can ever really eliminate it completely.

For example, during your dissertation defense, you'd have to be dead not to feel any stress. It's completely natural to feel even a little stress, and the tips given, as well as other tips, help reduce this stress.

However, for the stress that you still feel, you will become acclimatized to it. That is perfectly natural.

For example, much of the stress you feel comes from doing something new. You don't know what to expect. The very act of doing it helps you now understand what to expect, which reduces the stress the next time you do it.

If you're feeling stressed, for example giving a conference presentation for the first time, just know that it's normal and the first time is always the hardest. Do it anyway and you'll be better for it afterward.

36. JOIN A UNION

If there is a union at your university for PhD students, specifically, then you should look to join. If there isn't one, find one for students in general.

The reason why is because unions are great if you ever run into problems. They not only have experience dealing with student problems, but also the muscle to help. This is not only helpful for your PhD, but also a huge emotional boost.

There is one caveat – know where their funding is coming from; some unions derive their funding solely from their members. While that means that you are ultimately paying to be a member, you are in a much better position than if the union gets funding from the university. This is because the union is more independent if it gets its funding from its members.

If it gets its funding from the university, then there is a greater chance that it won't represent you in earnest if you need help.

37. BE KIND TO YOURSELF

Your head is where you live, so you should make it a nice place to be.

The quality of your thoughts eventually dictates the quality of your life because the nicer you are to yourself, the more belief you will have in yourself, and the more capable you will become.

The opposite trend also occurs.

At the end of the day, when it comes to assessing your own self worth, there's only one question that you need to answer and that is, "Did I do my best?"

If the answer is, "Yes", then you should be happy with yourself. The reason why is because the PhD process is about developing all kinds of skills, both professionally and personally.

It's astoundingly uncommon for someone to go through the PhD process without experiencing self-development.

As such, a PhD is not about doing things correctly. It's about learning how to do things correctly. And as long as you do your best, then there is no chance of not learning how to do things correctly.

So, remember to cut yourself some slack and be kind to yourself.

You'll see major benefits in the long run.

38. MAKE FRIENDS!

As mentioned in tip #34, looking at any dissertation acknowledgements will make it immediately obvious that the people who are part of your PhD help so much. And the help is not always on the technical side. In fact, much of the help you get from other people is more in the emotional form (as evidenced by these acknowledgement sections).

It's these people who will fill you with hope and positivity when things look bad.

Just simply being around people you like will help you.

One major source of happiness is other PhD students around you.

Every PhD student wants friends, even if they don't seem very open to begin with. But, deep down, everyone wants friends during their PhD.

Make friends with other PhD students so you always have people to be around when at university. What's more, these people understand exactly what you're thinking and feeling at any point during your PhD because they're going through it too.

You'll be surprised how much better your friends will make the grad school experience.

39. ATTEND CONFERENCES AND TALKS

Attending, and even presenting at conferences, is a hugely important part of your PhD.

Some of the major benefits of doing so include,

- Making a name for yourself
- Meeting other researchers in your field
- Learning how to communicate your research to others
- Seeing a new part of the world
- Learning about other aspects of your field and even neighboring fields
- Free food

As long as you take the right frame of mind into a conference or talk, you will gain much out of it. That frame of mind is to meet new people and learn about their work.

Too many people see conferences as just a way to further their careers, and in some ways it is. But, it's all to easy to forget that the people you're trying to use to further your career are PEOPLE too. They each have their own desires to further their careers too.

As such, going there with a very self-serving attitude of just trying to further your career doesn't work. The far better approach is to go there to make friends. Yes, I said, "friends".

Your goal is not to line up a job at that conference. Your goal is to meet people who will help you get a job, directly or indirectly, in the future, but only after you actually have a good relationship with them.

To give you an idea of what trying to get a job at a conference is like, imagine walking randomly up to someone on the street and inviting them over for dinner. Would the person say yes? Almost certainly not. They don't know you.

So, what does a conference do?

A conference facilitates the meeting of people in your field. From there, you can keep in touch and build relationships with them.

To give you a personal experience, I have never been offered a job at a conference. I have, however, been offered several jobs from people I met at conferences and stayed in contact with afterward.

How do you meet people at conferences?

The answer is incredibly obvious and simple – it's hiding in plain sight; if you want to meet someone, simply go up to them, politely introduce yourself, and say that you were reading their work or were in their talk and liked it. Then start elaborating on it, why you liked it, what questions you might have, and what you do.

It's as simple as that. There's no awkwardness doing that because that is what everyone is there for. You're not asking them to give you a job, you just want to meet them. That's very socially acceptable and amenable.

40. TRY TO ATTEND A CONFERENCE EVERY YEAR

Attending just one conference during your PhD is good, but if you can attend one every year, then you should do so. The reason is because you will often see the same faces at different conferences so you'll be able to better build relationships with these people.

Attending a conference every year can be expensive, especially if you have to travel internationally. However, with the advent of virtual conferences, you can attend them much more cheaply.

While virtual conferences are not as effective for networking, they are still better than nothing. And with the reduced cost, you can attend more of them to make up for the reduced effectiveness while still keeping the overall cost down.

Another added benefit for attending conferences regularly is that you can use this as an opportunity to email your network to see if they are going. A simple email asking a connection is a highly effective way of building your relationship as well as potentially setting a time to meet up at the conference, if they are going as well. Regardless of whether they are going or not, it's just a very effective way to touch base with them and keep in contact. This last point is a very underutilized approach to maintaining and strengthening your network.

41. NETWORK!

Speaking of networking in tip #40, we come to networking itself.

As much as we all might hate the idea that it's not what you know but who you know, unfortunately it's true. It's who you know. Evidence of this can be readily seen by the number of technically incompetent people in higher positions at universities and companies. They didn't get to where they are because they were the best at the technical side. They got to where they are because they were the best at networking.

To understand why networking is what determines how far you go, let's take an everyday example.

Say you were to buy a new phone. If you're like most people, you'll probably choose from among the well-known brands like Apple, Samsung, Huawei, etc. Why would you choose from these brands? It's quite simple – because you're not aware of any other brands. It could really be the case that there are other brands out there that make better phones, and cheaper. But, you are unaware of them, so how could you choose from them?

By default, the brands you know are the ones that will get chosen.

Likewise, when a job opening comes up, who do you think will get chosen, someone whom the hirer is aware of or someone whom the hirer isn't aware of? Obviously, the hirer cannot pick someone they aren't even aware of. That's where networking comes into play – by virtue of the fact that you're simply known, you immediately have a MASSIVE advantage. What's more, if the hirer has known for a while, that's an even bigger advantage because they are more comfortable with you; if the hirer has to choose between you and someone they don't know personally, then there will be all kinds of questions about this unknown person's personality traits, skills, and approach to work. You, on the other hand, pose fewer questions – the hirer knows you, so they know some of your personality traits, skills, and even approach to work. Hence, the hirer will be far more comfortable with hiring you. Once again, because of your networking skills, you have a MASSIVE advantage.

The better your networking skills, the more the positions will automatically be yours.

42. LOOK FOR COLLABORATIONS

Afantastic way to build your network is to look for collaborations. Collaborations between people in your department, or even university, are good, but collaborations with people outside of your university (your immediate circle) are even better.

There are so many benefits to collaborations. The first is the obvious networking benefit.

The second is that you can use the resources of two research groups instead of just one.

The third is that you now have even more expertise to draw from.

The fourth is that you become even more well-known in your field because your papers will typically become better, and hence more highly regarded.

The fifth is that you learn how to collaborate and organize workloads with distant people.

The sixth is that you might even get to visit your collaborators. If they live in a nice place, then the trip will be very enjoyable.

There are some downsides to collaboration, such as the increased logistical difficulty with organizing more people. However, the upsides usually far outweigh the downsides.

To set up a collaboration, use your network. Use colleagues of colleagues to get in touch. If you don't have any of these avenues, then you can always cold email other researchers in your field, but the difficulty of getting a, "yes" increases because of the unfamiliarity with you. This is just one more reason why your initial network is so important.

43. ORGANIZE YOUR PAPER'S AUTHOR ORDER EARLY

Every time you are planning a paper with your coauthors, make sure everyone knows what their roles in the paper writing process will be and what the authorship order will be.

This is incredibly important because, to put it bluntly, it reduces the chances of someone getting screwed over (I've been on the receiving end of this and it doesn't feel good).

If you cannot agree on the terms of the authorship order before you start working on the paper, then don't start working on the paper because it will likely end in tears.

Ideally, the terms of the authorship order should be decided even before the research has been conducted.

Above, I deliberately mentioned, "the terms of the authorship order" and not, "the authorship order". These are two different things. The first is a set of rules that determine what the authorship order will be. The second is what the authorship order is.

It's better to specify the terms instead of the actual authorship order because a paper is written, and published, over several months, and often years. Many things could happen in that time. For example, someone could move universities and now has less of an input. Under this circumstance, if they were given second authorship to begin with, they now get second authorship without putting in the work needed to be the second author.

On the other hand, if you specify the terms required to be second author and this person moves to another university, then their name in the order will still reflect the level of input they give.

Specifying the terms required for each position in the order reduces the amount of arguing and difficult conversations had at the end.

44. PRESENT "NEGATIVE" FINDINGS

"Negative" findings are where the results don't confirm your initial hypothesis, or possibly even show anything. These results are just as important as "positive" findings because they show other researchers what you found. They may have other ideas that come from this or just be thankful that they now know.

Negative findings are not bad, they're actually good. They are beneficial for a range of reasons from adding valuable knowledge to the field, to minimizing the wastage of resources spent on the same questions by other researchers, to reducing the pressure for academics to massage their findings to make them easier to publish.

There is a stigma that negative findings are bad because they are hard to get accepted for publication. That is true, but it is definitely not impossible to get them published. In fact, once you understand how to approach journals with your paper, it is surprisingly easy to get them published. In our book, "How To Write An Academic Paper 101", we cover in detail how to do this. (https://phdvoice.org/product/writing-an-academic-paper-101/)

45. WEAR COMFORTABLE CLOTHES

This may seem like a ridiculous tip, but it is very important. People who are comfortable are happier than people who aren't comfortable. Happier people are more motivated.

Wear comfortable clothes. It will have a positive long-term effect.

46. MAKE YOUR WORKING ENVIRONMENT COMFORTABLE

In addition to wearing comfortable clothes (tip #45), you need to have a comfortable working environment.

This covers everything from noise, to lighting, to your chair, to your computer setup.

For example, the blue light coming from your computer can make it very difficult to sleep at night because our melatonin levels become affected and that alters our circadian rhythm ("bodyclock"). This makes it harder to sleep when you should be sleep.

Another example of how comfort affects our productivity is how often you get interrupted. We might like to believe that being interrupted is bad, but we can refocus very quickly. This is wrong. The data on this topic is still emerging, but estimates indicate that every time we get interrupted, it takes 5 minutes for us to get back into the same concentration level we were before the interruption. Some data indicates that it takes much longer, like 20 minutes.

So, if you're getting interrupted every 10 minutes, then you are only working at full efficiency 50% of the time. Half your day is at full efficiency, the other half is struggling along.

47. USE THE "NIGHTSHIFT" FUNCTION ON YOUR DEVICES

To overcome the problems with sleep presented in tip #46, a very good approach is to use the "nightshift" function on your devices, not just your computer.

This nightshift reduces the amount of blue light we see, and hence normalizes our circadian rhythm.

However, the nightshift also helps reduce the strain on our eyes.

For example, how many times have you woken up in the middle of the night, wondered to yourself what time it is, then rolled over, picked up your phone, turned it on to see the time, only to have all this white light burning right into your eyeballs?

You immediately think, "Why did I do that!", as you roll around in bed trying to come to terms with the fact that this is the third time this week you fell for that trick. Then you start wondering if you're even smart enough to do a PhD (tip #16). Then you finally decide that there's no hope left and quit.

Well, if you've ever had that sensation, nightshift will reduce it – depending on the level you set, it could completely eliminate the sensation completely.

And that is how nightshift will stop you from quitting your PhD...it will also help balance your sleeping pattern.

48. EAT WELL

Eating well is vital not only for your health, but for all aspects of your life.

Eating healthily leads to more energy and better long-term focus. The reason why is because healthy foods not only have the right nutrients, they also get released into our bodies (which have evolved to suit these foods) at sustainable rates.

For example, did you know that a banana has almost as much sugar in it as Coca Cola. That's not the big deal though. The big deal is that the speed at which energy is released from Coca Cola is about 25% faster than a banana (and Coca Cola is quite slow compared to other junk food). This results in mood swings because the faster that energy is released, the faster it is gone, which results in spikes in moods.

Mood swings result in instabilities in emotional, mental, and physical states. For example, it is very common for people to feel like "imposters" during their PhDs. This feeling is an emotional state. If, for example, you eat something with a very high energy release speed (a high glycemic index), you will get an emotional high. When the energy is all used up, you get an emotional low. That low makes it very easy to feel down about everything, including your self-image. In other words, this low can, and does, feed your imposter syndrome. Yes, there are other factors contributing to the imposter syndrome, but it starts with emotional stability. Emotional stability is heavily influenced by the foods and drinks we consume.

Make sure you eat healthily.

49. DON'T FORGET TO HAVE FUN!

The word "fun" is often forgotten when we do a PhD, and in life in general. We have so many other things to do that we forget sometimes.

It's vital for morale to keep having fun.

The important thing to realize is that you don't need to wait until you're doing something just for yourself (tip #20) or taking a break (tip #99) to have fun.

It's not only possible, but recommended to have fun with your research.

How many times have you been doing your research only to wonder what would happen if you changed something about it?

Sometimes, you definitely cannot fulfil this fantasy, but other times you definitely can. In those times, just do it. See what happens. Who knows, you might find something interesting.

What's more, you're building fun into your research.

50. FIND AN EXERCISE ROUTINE THAT WORKS FOR YOU

Exercise is one of the most important aspects of your entire life. Without it, you can't expect to be healthy. You can't expect to naturally feel good. We'll talk a little more about the mental benefits of exercise in tip #92, however, the obvious physical benefits include not getting sick as often. And when you get sick, you also recover quicker. You sleep better. Your default mood is a good one. You are happier.

One major unsung benefit of exercise is that it boosts your confidence. It's very common for people to feel like "imposters" during their PhDs, however, one point that is often overlooked is how your life outside of your PhD (and you should definitely have a life outside of your PhD) affects your PhD life. Achieving something outside of your PhD will make you feel more confident. That confidence will follow you into your PhD as well, whether you consciously try to bring it or not. Either way, you'll feel more confident.

Confidence is nothing more than feeling capable. You believe that you can do something. Exercise is a challenge and every time you exercise, you overcome it. It's hard not to feel confident when you do that, especially on a regular basis.

So, in your daily plan (tip #27), make sure to schedule in time to exercise. Exercise regularly. At least once per week. As a side note, if you have health issues, consult your doctor for exercises that you can do.

51. SET ASIDE TIME EACH DAY FOR RELAXATION

In addition to exercising regularly (tip #50), set aside time to relax every single day.

Have you ever had the sensation of the days just flying by and before you know it, whole months and even years have just passed?

Much of that comes from being so busy that we don't even register what we're doing. We just keep going.

Taking time out every day to reflect (tip #21) and relax breaks up your day. It prevents you getting so caught up with other things that you forget to appreciate your life.

To relax, you can pick anything that calms you. It should be calming because you can do that regardless of what kind of day you've had and no matter how exhausted you are. For example, a form of unwinding might be wrestling a bear for some people, but if you're really tired, you might not feel in the mood to do that today. So, they're sitting at work, thinking, "I have scheduled in for my relaxation to wrestle a bear today, but I'm not feeling up to it. Oh well...I'll just skip it and work instead".

Big mistake! Don't skip your daily relaxation time.

On the other hand, if you just do something that calms you, regardless of how little energy you have, you can still do it.

52. GET ENOUGH SLEEP

We've covered in several tips how to improve your sleep (tips #46, #47, and #50), however, we haven't touched upon the nuanced tip of actually getting enough sleep.

Everyone needs different amounts of sleep. What's more, each person's sleep needs changes from day to day and even from season to season. In winter, we require more sleep than in summer.

Learn to listen to your body and follow what it's telling you. The less sleep you get, the less efficient you are when working.

If you need 9 hours of sleep per night, then do everything you can to get those 9 hours. If you need 6, then get 6.

53. TRY NOT TO COMPARE YOURSELF WITH OTHERS

Comparing yourself with others during your PhD, and even life, is almost second nature. But don't do it.

One of the major reasons why we compare ourselves with others during our PhDs is because we are unsure about the process. The PhD process is very long and there's so much to it. We feel uncertain. So, if we see someone else doing something, we want to know.

What's more, if we see someone else fulfilling a criterion for their PhD, we feel like we're being left behind and we need to catch up.

It's perfectly normal to feel like this, but it's also very counterproductive.

Let me give you an example. When I first started my PhD, I had a very close friend who also started his at the same time. Because of his past experience with research, he was already well ahead of where I was in terms of development.

As such, while I was spending the first few months endlessly reading so I could do my literature review, he was already starting his research campaign and collecting data.

I felt like I had just started and I was somehow already well behind.

Guess what happened?

We finished within 1 month of each other by the end.

His "head start" made no difference in the end.

Why?

Because each PhD path is a little different. We all learn at different rates. What's more, we all learn different things. Yes, we all learn the core traits to be good researchers, however, there is so much more that we learn.

No two people will follow the exact same timeline.

Don't worry if you feel like you're behind. The best thing to do is to ignore it, say to yourself, "I'm just going to do my thing at my pace". Everything will work out.

I, and many other people like me, am proof of that.

54. DON'T LOSE SIGHT OF WHAT YOU'RE HERE FOR

Answer question, "What are you doing your PhD for?"

Be completely honest. List what you're here for. It could be as simple as, "I'm here to get my PhD", or more complicated like, "I'm here to get my PhD, get teaching experience, network, etc."

Whatever you're here for, burn that into your mind.

It's important to do that because it will be your guiding star.

Any time something pops up during your working hours, that you could do, assess whether it fits your goal or not. If it does, then do it. If it doesn't then don't do it.

It's as simple as that.

55. REMEMBER THAT YOU'RE NOT ALONE

The PhD experience is a lonely one, so it can feel like no one has ever gone through what you're going through. But don't forget that there are plenty of people who have been where you are right now, and they made it through just fine—and so will you!

Remember in tip #53 where I covered how my friend seemed so much further ahead than me when we both started? Do you know what I did? I just kept asking him questions. I understood that he knew so much more than me about research, and even our fields, that I knew that I could learn from him.

In fact, I asked him so many questions that if we weren't such good friends, he probably would've asked me to stop asking him so many questions. But he didn't.

However, I was prepared in the event that he would ask me to stop – I knew a dozen other PhD students and a bunch of other postdocs and other researchers I could ask questions if my friend got tired of my incessant questioning.

What's more, if he did ask me to stop, I would've pointed out that his teaching me was benefiting his learning too (tip #30).

Everyone is okay with you asking questions or just simply

hanging around for some company because everyone is going through the same thing, or they have gone through the same thing.

56. DON'T GET DISCOURAGED BY THE LONG ROAD AHEAD OF YOU

As tip #55 points out, everyone is going through the same thing. I don't think there is a person who has ever been 100% motivated throughout their entire PhD.

At some point, you will wake up one morning and just want to roll over instead of getting up and going to university.

It's completely normal. This feeling is also compounded when you look at how much further you have to go.

So, this tip is to not get discouraged.

This is probably the hardest tip to do in this entire book.

There is nothing that will work for everyone, but one way that works for me is to find a quote about keeping going that you always rest on when you feel discouraged.

Mine is a very famous quote. It's,

> "If you're going through hell, keep going."

I read this quote every time I feel like quitting. I also have it stuck to my wall where I read it every day. It also makes me laugh (tip #57).

If it doesn't work for you, then find another quote that does. There are many and some work better for you than others.

57. FIND A WAY TO LAUGH EVERY DAY!

One of the most powerful things you can do for yourself is to laugh.

Genuinely laughing has so many benefits.

It greatly reduces stress and helps you feel better about whatever is going on in your life.

It helps you bond with others – making friends (tip #38) is so much easier when you like to laugh and joke around. People gravitate toward that and the longer your PhD goes, the more of a shining beacon it will be for others.

Laughing also helps put things in perspective for you; if you can still find something to laugh about, then whatever has happened can't be that bad and there is still hope.

58. CELEBRATE EVERY LITTLE WIN

PhDs are a long journey, taking years.

It's difficult to stay motivated and encouraged throughout the entire thing. However, one very effective way to do so is by celebrating every little win.

If you think of just the overall goal of getting your PhD, then it's a very long time to go without feeling like you've achieved something.

If you break down your tasks (tip #18), each time you accomplish one, make sure to celebrate it.

It could be as simple as taking a few minutes off and going to chat with a friend.

By celebrating every win, no matter how small the accomplishment is, you get a little bit of motivation and confidence every time.

To help with this, we often tweet out asking people to list some wins, big or small. If you like, you can keep an eye out for when we do this. In addition, you can set a time every week where you recap what you achieved, and even do so with friends so you build a positive group (tip #81).

59. ACCEPT THAT YOU DID YOUR BEST

One of the hardest things to come to terms with is when something doesn't work out. It could be a failed experiment, or a paper being rejected.

If you did your best, then that's all you can ask for. At the end of the day, you won't get everything right the first time you try. That's the whole point of doing a PhD. You learn from mistakes.

The only thing you can really control is how much effort you put into it. If you put all your effort into something and it still doesn't work out, then that's nothing to be unhappy about. You did your best.

One caveat that must be teased out is that doing your best doesn't mean that you work 24 hours per day for 7 days straight on something because that's technically not your best – you have other tasks to do, so the more you spend on one task, the less you can spend on another task. What's more, the more you run yourself down now, the less energy you will have in the future. As such, doing your best is about sustainability. Don't sacrifice your future energy levels for an additional boost of energy now because if you do that, then you can't do your best in the future because you'll be too tired.

60. LEARN FROM YOUR MISTAKES

Mistakes are fantastic things. They give you the opportunity to learn.

The only thing is that you need to make sure you learn from them.

The sooner you learn from your mistake, the better off you'll be.

As such, much of your PhD is not really about how many things you get right, but how quickly you recover from making a mistake, learning from it, and moving on.

Learn from your mistakes.

61. LEARN FROM THE MISTAKES OF OTHERS

In addition to learning from your own mistakes (tip #60), learning from other people's mistakes is of great importance.

Think about how much time and effort it took to make your mistake and then learn from it. Say you made a mistake in your research...well, it probably took you months of planning that research. That means that that mistake took months to do and hence months to learn from.

On the other hand, if you observe other people, you can learn from their mistakes – that is far more efficient. They have put in those months of hard work and you can learn from their mistakes within only a few moments.

You can learn from all kinds of people and in all kinds of fashions. For example, you could talk with a friend about their research. You could also read a book – each time you read a book, you are learning from the author(s) experience and mistakes. These are very efficient ways of learning.

62. DON'T BE AFRAID TO ADMIT THAT YOU'RE WRONG, EVEN TO YOURSELF

Much of the difficulty that arises during the PhD process, and in academia in general, arises from when you can't admit to yourself that you're wrong about something.

This comes in all forms. For example, when a debate occurs and one side is clearly wrong, but they cannot admit it. Or, when you know that there is a mistake in something, but you hope for the best instead of fixing it.

Research is not about being right, it's about finding the answer. Hypotheses don't have to be right. All that has to be correct is the method you used. The answer you end up getting is kind of superfluous. The only thing that matters is that it is the correct answer. If it isn't, then you need to admit that and determine where to go from there.

In our book, "How To Write An Academic Paper 101" (https://phdvoice.org/product/writing-an-academic-paper-101/), we go through, in detail, how to handle this and how to accurately write your results in a paper that will still get published.

63. WHEN A MISTAKE OR PROBLEM IS DISCOVERED, ACCEPT IT AND DON'T TRY TO HIDE IT

Akin to tip #62, don't try to hide mistakes.

Mistakes happen, and that's part of the PhD process – you're there to learn. Surprisingly, almost every piece of research can be salvaged to some extent.

The main way to do this is to simply think about what question our research now addresses.

It may be that your research is not going to be as encompassing any more. Perhaps you have to make some assumptions now to mitigate the weaknesses. If so, that's fine. Just say so and put in your future work how assessing those assumptions would be of interest.

What's more, don't try to hide problems. Be as transparent as possible. It just isn't worth it from an ethical point of view and from a career point of view.

In fact, other researchers love when you are honest about the flaws in your work. They even hold you up as an example of the type of researcher everyone should be – one with integrity. Academia can never get enough of that.

64. CONDUCT YOUR RESEARCH THOROUGHLY

Acorollary to tip #63 is to conduct your research thoroughly. If you can see that something about your research may become a problem later on, whether that's the method you've selected, or the question, or even the data processing approach, fix it now! Don't wait because the longer you wait, the bigger the problem becomes.

The ability to do this also stems from tips #10 and #11 where making plans and keeping them up-to-date helps you understand what needs to be done next, why, and what potential problems you will face.

The good news is that the more experienced you get, the easier it becomes to spot problems. So, at the start, use the expertise of your supervisors to see what potential problems there are. Some questions you should ask are:

- What resources do I need?
- Do I have access to these resources?
- Will this method answer the question I have?
- What will be the uncertainty of my results?

- Will this uncertainty be acceptable?

65. GET YOUR FRIENDS AND COLLEAGUES TO HELP YOU SPOT POTENTIAL PROBLEMS IN YOUR RESEARCH

Acorollary to that last tip is that when you've scrutinized your research plan and cannot find any potential problems, then run it by other knowledgeable people (not just your supervisors but even your friends who know about your field) to see if they can see any problems.

Almost every PhD student has been helped by other researchers during their PhDs. That's the goal – to build a group where you can get help when you need it and give help when someone else needs it.

It all starts with asking.

One thing that can hold people back from helping is the question of who will get credit for the research.

Unfortunately, credit in academia is the equivalent of gold. Often people will be reluctant to help you because they will feel like they won't get credit for their input. Likewise, people may be reluctant to ask for help because they will feel like they will need to give some credit to the person who helped.

Every working relationship is different and it is something that should be figured out explicitly – everyone should be clear about the credit they will receive before help is given. The reason why is because it prevents a very messy situation later on.

The best working relationships I've ever had were, and are, with my close friends. The agreement that we've always come to is that we will help solve problems and give ideas, but we don't expect to be included in the author list – acknowledgement is adequate. We arrived at this arrangement because it removes the boundaries restricting us from asking for help – there is no concern about having an author list as long as our arms. Also, in our field, this is an acceptable ethical standpoint to adopt – if you haven't written anything, then you are not an author. Your field may be different, which is why you can check and use that to help guide your working relationships.

66. COMMIT TO YOUR PLAN

So, you've thoroughly analyzed your plan. You've gotten your supervisors to do the same. You've even gotten your colleagues to assess it to.

Once you've done that and everything seems fine, go forward with it. It's easy to feel like you're missing something or just fear the worst, but if you've done everything you can to find potential errors, then it's time to move forward with your plan.

Commit to it and only use the regular time you set aside to go over your plan (tip #11) to question it. For the rest of the time, follow it without hesitation. This will make you more focused on what you're doing, both when you're carrying out your research and going over your plan periodically.

67. LEARN HOW TO DEAL WITH REJECTION

Rejections will happen during your PhD. You cannot escape them.

Everyone gets rejected. So, don't feel like you're not good enough.

But that is only one of the reasons why people get so deflated why they're rejected.

The other reason is because you feel like you've put all this effort in and it has been wasted. The hope you had is now gone.

That is a very demotivating feeling because when you put in effort and it doesn't pay off, you feel like there's no point to trying again because there's no hope.

To overcome this feeling, think of your PhD as a path. There are highs and lows. The thing that matters most is that you keep trying. This is because as long as you keep trying, the highs and lows will start to average out and the slope of your path will be positive. In other words, you will keep moving up over time...as long as you keep trying.

The highs and lows average out over time.

68. BE OPEN TO CONSTRUCTIVE FEEDBACK

Criticism, in general, sucks. No one likes having holes poked in their work.

But, constructive criticism is much better...at least it's helpful.

However, it can still be difficult to stomach because each hole poked in your work feels like your chances of finishing your PhD are being undermined.

One thing to keep in mind when you feel like this is that a PhD is not actually about the work you put out. It's actually about how much you learn and how competent you become as a researcher. It is absurd to think that something you do at the start of your PhD should be perfect. If it is, then your PhD has been a waste of your time because you were already a competent researcher!

Yes, by the end of your PhD, you should be a competent research, but that is at the END. And a competent researcher is capable of looking back at previous work and finding ways to improve upon it, especially if that work was conducted by someone still learning how to research.

Anyone who loses sight of the fact that the earlier work of a PhD student should be flawed, has lost sight of what a PhD is actually about. It's about taking a person of a certain level and training him/her to be a competent researcher.

So, if a hole is exposed, that's fine. The only thing you need to do is learn why it came about and what you would do differently next time. As for the papers that could be written, just brainstorm with your supervisors how this problem can be compensated for or overcome in the write up.

69. BE OPEN TO CHANGE

Like in tips #62 and #63, sometimes things will happen that force you to change.

It can be hard to come to terms with it because you might feel a whole range of emotions from not feeling adequate because your PhD is turning into a "failure", to feeling deflated because you have to do all of this additional work now.

While you might feel these emotions, I mean this in the nicest possible way, you're wrong. :)

You are a PhD student, you're not all-knowing. You're not a research guru...yet. You're there to learn.

Any problem that arises is actually caused by someone else other than you.

I know this sounds cowardly because you are passing the blame onto someone else, but it's not cowardly because in this particular instance, it's true.

As long as you do your best, then you are not responsible.

Your supervisor, for example, should have assessed your abilities better so that s/he could assign more suitable tasks, or even someone to help you.

Once you've overcome these emotions, the next step is to accept that change has to happen, whether that means your research question has to change, or your method, or anything else that is currently holding you back.

Whatever is wrong is holding you back and the only way forward is by changing it.

To understand just how important it is to accept, and even embrace, change when it is necessary, this is a quote from Charles Darwin:

> *It is not the strongest of the species that survives, not the most intelligent that survives. It is the one that is the <u>most adaptable to change</u>.*

70. IT'S OKAY IF THINGS AREN'T GOING EXACTLY HOW YOU WANT THEM TO GO

APhD is all about learning how to do research effectively, and while it would be nice if everything went to plan, it's probably not going to.

However, managing the emotions you'll feel when something doesn't go to plan can be difficult. The first thing to do is to understand what you're feeling and why.

One of the strongest emotions is general is dejection. When we put so much energy into something and it doesn't work out how we wanted it to, we naturally feel deflated. Along with that comes a lack of belief that we can truly reach our goal. And when we don't truly believe that we can reach our goal, then our motivation plummets.

Another very strong emotion we feel when things don't go

wrong is a lack of belief in the rest of our plan (tips #10 and #11). We feel like what we have done already, which was part of our plan, didn't go well so what are the chances that the rest will go well. This feeling is akin to the other emotion we just covered, but it is slightly different in that with this emotion we have a lack of trust in our plan, while the previous emotion, there was just a general lack of trust, including in our own abilities.

Once again, this feeling is perfectly normal and remember that we mentioned that plans aren't useful in that everything goes to plan, but they are useful in that they make you think about what needs to be done and in what order.

Another strong emotion is panic because you may feel like you're now behind schedule and won't finish your PhD. That is a possibility – some things just don't follow their schedule. However, it's important not to panic, even now, because panic often results in even more mistakes. For example, you may quickly schedule a new experiment to make up for your old one, but in so doing, there may be a foreseeable flaw in it (because of your haste) and that uses resources and puts you even further behind.

For some people, there is no such thing as "behind" because they're happy to take as long as needed to finish their PhDs. For other people, there is such a thing as "behind". If you happen to be one of those people who believe that there is such a thing as "behind", then that's perfectly fine and understandable, however, don't panic. Just take some time to think about what happened, why it happened, and even if you can still salvage it. Many times, you can salvage what you have.

All of these feelings you feel during setbacks are perfectly normal so just understand what they are and why you are feeling them. Then remember that these feelings and events are to be expected and 99.99% of people who have ever finished their PhDs have had things go wrong and they still finished. I personally don't know any PhD holder who had their PhD go 100% to plan, and I know thousands of PhD holders.

In fact, when you think about what it means to be good at research, it entails the ability to bounce back after a setback. So, you can argue that if you never learn this skill, then your PhD wasn't a true success because after your PhD, you will definitely encounter setbacks and it's far better to experience setbacks during your PhD where you're in a controlled environment than for the first time later when you have even more riding on the line.

71. MAKE SURE YOU KEEP UP WITH YOUR READING

As we all know, a PhD takes place over several years, and unfortunately it's not like your entire field freezes for that period of time while you can do your research and publish it.

During those years, your field will continue to develop with new research being published every day.

Keeping up with it not only helps you keep your research relevant, but it also improves your understanding of your field. Who knows, maybe something you read during that time will trigger a profound idea in you that will help you better interpret your results. In fact, this occurrence is more likely than not.

In addition to keeping up with the reading in your field, it is highly beneficial to read neighboring fields, and even very different fields. You'd be surprised how much you can learn AND use in your own research from what you learn about different fields.

For example, some fields are incredibly advanced in their error/uncertainty analysis. Some fields are terrible. If you're in a field that has a very infantile grasp of error analysis, then imagine how well your research will be received if you start incorporating a good error analysis? You will be setting a new standard and be seen as a "whizz kid"...even if you're a mature-age student. ;)

Keep up with the latest research in your own field and also read other fields as much as you can. You never know what useful information you'll find until you read it.

72. GO TO CLASS OFTEN

I was recently talking to a PhD student who had some exams coming up. He was incredibly stressed out about them. So much so that he took an entire month off just to study before the exams...not to mention the addition couple of weeks during the exam period between the exams that he had.

During this 6 week period, he didn't have time to do anything else on his PhD. What's more, he was very tired from so much studying.

It turned out that he hadn't been going to classes very often. He had the idea that he would not physically go to class, but instead, he would watch the recordings online.

That was a big mistake.

Because he could access the recordings at any time in the future, he kept forgetting to watch the recordings. As such, when the end of the semester rolled around, he hadn't watched many lectures and had to spend that whole month prior to the exams just learning, for the first time, the material in the classes.

Because there was no urgent need for him to go to class, he didn't.

It might seem like a good idea to save the travel time and just stay home or be somewhere else, and watch the recordings later, but this good intention very easily goes awry.

By having the impetus to physically go to class, you make sure you do. Don't think that you will catch up, because life has a way of throwing more tasks at us and before we know it, it's exam time and we know nothing about the material yet.

So, make sure you physically go to class.

Note: During this friend's semester, his university did not have any "social distancing" restrictions.

73. TAKE NOTES IN CLASS AND REVIEW THEM LATER

In addition to going to class, make sure you take notes.

This is a fine line to tread because research shows that we remember much more when we write the information down as oppose to sitting and just listening.

The problem is that, the more you write, the more your head is down in your book and the less attention you can pay to the lecturer – you're learning very advanced stuff and you need a good amount of brainpower to comprehend it. If some of that brainpower is being syphoned off to write notes, then your comprehension levels drop.

As such, it's important to take notes, but know when your note taking is reducing the amount you are taking in to begin with.

What's more, if you are taking notes and you happen to miss something the lecturer said, ask her/him to repeat it.

74. ASK QUESTIONS IN CLASS, EVEN IF THEY SEEM STUPID OR POINTLESS

Following on from tip #73, make sure to ask any and every question you have.

One reason why people don't ask questions is because they fear that their classmates will think that they're stupid.

There are two reasons not to care. The first is that your classmates can be divided into two groups – those who know you and those who don't. Those who know you are not going to base their opinion of you on a question you ask. They know you better than that.

As for those who don't know you, well, they're not really doing anything for you anyway, so who cares what they think? If they're superficial enough to judge someone on a question they asked, especially if that person is just trying to learn, then they're not worth worrying about.

The second reason why people often feel scared of asking

questions is because they fear what the lecturer will think of them.

If you've ever lectured before, you know that someone asking you something is very nice because it means that you actually have someone who is engaged. The far worse thing is when you have a bunch of students who missed what you said, but are too afraid to ask.

Personally, I love when students ask me questions because it means that they're interacting and want to learn. If I don't get any questions, then I start to feel uneasy because there's a chance that they're just not paying attention.

So, don't be afraid to ask questions.

75. DON'T BE AFRAID TO TALK TO PEOPLE

In addition to asking the lecturer questions, ask your classmates and people who have taken the class in previous semesters.

Many people will be happy to help you because they know what it's like to not understand something.

As for those who find it annoying, most will still help, albeit begrudgingly. Don't worry about their attitudes because most of these people are overestimating just how well they know what you're asking. You'll find this too if you just keep asking questions about anything you're not sure about. Sooner or later, you'll ask them something that s/he doesn't know and s/he will end up happy that you asked because you highlighted something they need to know more about, AND they will no longer think that you're stupid because you saw something they didn't. How do I know that they don't know everything about the subject? Because they're not getting 100%.

So, just ask questions. Many of them.

76. FIND SOMEONE YOU CAN TRUST AND LEAN ON THEM WHEN YOU NEED HELP (OR JUST NEED A FRIEND)

Most people doing a PhD will feel the exact same things as you.

As some point, they'll feel happy, sad, elated, frustrated, calm, angry, hopeful, dejected, grateful, ungrateful, smart, stupid, and more!

You're not the first person to feel any of these things during your PhD, and you won't be the last.

If you have friends in your PhD cohort, make sure to share these emotions with them because they might be able to help you when you need help. As for the positive emotions, they'll be happy because you're bringing some positivity to them, as well.

You don't necessarily need to approach your friends in your PhD cohort – you can always use your friends outside, as well. We forget about the outside world, but just spending time with friends not in academia helps us put into perspective our problems. There is a life outside of academia.

77. YOU CAN NEVER KNOW TOO MUCH ABOUT YOUR FIELD

Similar to tips #14 and #71, you can never know too much about your field.

It's common for PhD students to stop learning about their fields after a certain point. One of the major reasons is that things are going well so there is less impetus to keep learning about your field.

I truly get this, but everything you learn during your PhD will help you after your PhD. So, while you may be knowledgeable enough to make it through your PhD, you are selling yourself short by not learning more because your life after your PhD will suffer.

78. DON'T FORGET THAT THIS IS A MARATHON, NOT A SPRINT

APhD is analogous to a marathon. It takes many years.

It is tempting to take a "sprint" mentality into a PhD because the harder you go, the faster you'll finish...right?

That's not quite true, and for a number of reasons.

The first is that going hard straight out of the gates is natural, but if you go too hard and push yourself for too long, you'll burnout.

Secondly, there are some processes in your PhD that cannot be sped up. For example, if you have a requirement that you need to publish at least one journal article in order to qualify for a PhD (which about 40% of PhD students have – according to our own Twitter polls), then the time it takes for your paper to go through the publication process is largely out of your control.

Your paper needs to be sent to the editor, but once it's there, it goes to reviewers, then back to the editor. All of these stages run on their own clocks.

As such, you cannot control the time it takes to get your paper published.

There are only two things you can control about the time taken. The first is the quality of your paper. The second is how quickly you submit your paper to a journal.

The higher the quality, the easier it will be to get it accepted, and hence the quicker it will be. (We have already mentioned a couple of times our book that teaches you how to write better papers and get them accepted more easily, "How To Write An Academic Paper 101", here, https://phdvoice.org/product/writing-an-academic-paper-101/).

The sooner you can get your paper written and sent off, the earlier in your PhD it will be accepted. To do this, you need to plan your PhD well (tips #10 and #11) and don't compromise on the quality of your paper because submitting a poorer quality paper sooner will not necessarily result in an earlier acceptance date.

79. UNDERSTAND YOUR BODY-CLOCK AND ABIDE BY IT

One of the greatest misunderstandings in the world, not just academia, is our body-clock.

We've covered in other tips (#46 and #47) how your body-clock can be affected by your working environment, but it is also affected by the day and time of year.

During summer, when the days are longer, we typically need less sleep and feel more energized. During winter, we want to sleep more and do less.

That's perfectly fine and you shouldn't override what your body is telling you. It's telling you that for a reason.

So, if you find that you're not being as productive, then ask yourself if it's because you don't feel as energized. If so, then it could be simply because your body-clock is putting on the brakes for now.

80. YOU WON'T LIKE YOUR SUPERVISOR ALL THE TIME, AND THAT'S OKAY

It's important to choose a good supervisor (tip #2), but even if you do, there will be times when you still won't like them. And that's okay because there are several reasons why you won't like them some of the time, and all of these normal reasons are fine.

One of the reasons is because your supervisor's job is to supervise you, but they also have other jobs to do. They might lecture or even supervise other students. So, they are juggling a bunch of other responsibilities. Sometimes, they might drop the ball – no one is perfect. The important thing is that they're trying and that they're not dropping the ball often. They might go through a bad period, but if it picks up again, then there is nothing to worry about. Changing supervisors won't likely improve your situation because everyone screws up occasionally, and as long as it is occasionally and not maliciously, then it's fine.

Another reason why you might dislike your supervisor at some point during your PhD is because there is this inextricable link between your progress and your supervisor. It's very tempting to think that your supervisor is responsible for any problems that arise during your PhD. They are for some, but for others, perhaps they are not because those problems were unforeseeable, out of their control, or the lesser of two evils. Despite this, we still feel a strong coupling between these problems and our supervisors.

Whenever you start to dislike your supervisor, it's important to take a step back and assess whether it is truly his/her fault or not. In some instances, it genuinely is. In others, it is not.

And in some cases, PhD students have picked bad supervisors (tip #2) and they would be better off if they switched supervisors to someone else.

81. SPEND AS MUCH TIME AS YOU CAN AROUND POSITIVE PEOPLE AND AS LITTLE TIME AS POSSIBLE AROUND NEGATIVE PEOPLE

One secret that we tend to forget as we get older is that you should try to control whom you spend time with. There are people whom you have to interact with regardless of whether you like it or not. However, there are some people whom you don't have to. And even those whom you do have to interact with, you can limit the amount of time you spend with them.

What's more, you can also find people who are good for you and spend more time with them.

The people you should minimize exposure to are the negative

people. These people have been labelled all sorts of things over the years, but one thing that they truly are, is just a bad influence on you. Negative people reduce your motivation because negativity robs you of your can-do attitude. If you have two people, one feels empowered and one feels disempowered, who do you think will accomplish more?

With all else being equal, the empowered person will. Negativity makes you feel disempowered. Positivity makes you feel empowered.

Identify those who are positive and those who are negative. As much as you can, hang around the positive people and not the negative people.

It may seem a little wrong to stop interacting with negative people, but it will serve you well in the long run. What's more, over time, other people will understand why you are avoiding the negative people and will support you in it.

At the end of the day, a PhD is a long road and the last thing you need is for your motivation to dive because of negative influences around you.

82. GIVE OTHER PEOPLE COMPLIMENTS ON THEIR WORK

One of the best ways to foster positive relationships (tip #81) is to give other people compliments on their work. You'd be surprised just how effective this is, and for two reasons.

The first reason is that giving people compliments helps you identify who is positive and who is negative; have you ever given someone a compliment only for them to say something negative and downtrodden? For example, "Yeah, but I still have all of these other things to do". This is a negative attitude.

On the other hand, have you ever given someone a compliment and they were thankful for it, for example, "Thanks! I'm happy with it too". This is a positive person.

Now you know whom you should hang around more and whom you shouldn't hang around so much.

The second reason why giving other people compliments is beneficial is because the positive people will return the goodwill later to you and that will help you feel good about your work as well. You might be surprised how grateful some people are that another person is supportive of them and they'll want to return the favor to continue the positive relationship, and build upon it.

83. DON'T LEAVE THINGS TO THE LAST MINUTE

When you first start your PhD, you will usually have only a couple of things to do. Maybe some reading for your literature review and a course to take.

But as you progress through your PhD, the number of things you have to do just starts multiplying; perhaps you'll still have some reading (tip #71), but you also have to analyze some data, plan another experiment, do some teaching (tip #31), take a course, write up that data, have a meeting with your supervisors, get ready for a conference, and remember to eat well (tip #48).

It's easy for things to snowball. As such, do your best to jump onto a task as soon as possible. The trick to this is to identify which tasks are worth doing and which ones are not (tip #28). Discard the tasks not worth doing and focus solely on the tasks worth doing.

This is so important because if you start leaving things until later, sooner or later, you'll have a bunch of tasks that need to be done NOW and you have no time to do them all. This leads to a feeling of being overwhelmed.

Now, this is life and unfortunately, there will be times, no matter how hard you try, where more than one thing needs to be done now. These things happen. However, you can minimize these occurrences by jumping onto tasks as soon as they pop up and not leaving them until some future date. And remember, this only goes for those tasks worth doing. Chewing your time up with those tasks not worth doing, like checking your emails every 30 minutes, is not a good idea.

84. SET BARRIERS FOR YOURSELF AND YOUR WORK

For example, at the bottom of your email, you can say that you only check your emails two times per day. Once at 9:00am and once at 4:00pm. If they need you urgently, they can call you. That way, you don't have to check your emails every 30 minutes and chew up time.

This is just one example, but many others exist. For example, you can set a barrier that you do not work past 5:30pm unless it is to use some resources that aren't available at other times. And if you do this, then credit yourself that time and turn up late the next day to compensate yourself.

Protect your time and yourself. If you do it politely and nicely, people will respect it and even support you in doing that...just make sure that you have first selected good supervisors (tip #2).

85. REMEMBER THAT YOU AREN'T THE ONLY ONE WHO FEELS THIS WAY, EVERYONE DOES

One of the most isolating aspects of a PhD is our incessant belief that no one else understands what we're feeling.

For example, we may have a paper rejected and while we know that everyone gets papers rejected sooner or later (and that's 100% true, by the way), that paper rejection was different for us because we needed that paper published to finish our PhD.

Well, many PhD students have felt this. And many PhD students have felt every other feeling you have had and will have.

And remember, you don't have to keep these feelings to yourself; you can tell friends, colleagues, and even the student counselling department at your university (tip #76).

86. GET PROPER SUNLIGHT EXPOSURE EVERY DAY

Getting enough sunlight every day is important because it controls our sleeping patterns. It's so common for PhD students to stay up late doing work, then fall asleep in the wee hours of the morning, wake up late, then repeat the whole thing again and again until they're eventually nocturnal.

One reason why this happens is because we feel like there is so much work to do and we need to do it. Another reason is because we might feel like we're more productive at night.

Whatever the reason is, it is unfortunately an unhealthy habit, and for two reasons.

The first reason is that there are countless studies showing that repeatedly sleeping during the day and working at night, over time, increases chances of a myriad diseases.

The second reason is that being nocturnal usually results in less sleep because you have to wake up early for a meeting or some other daytime activity. Less sleep results in poorer health.

Along with these health problems, over time you become less

productive because you have less sleep.

To regulate our sleep, sun exposure is paramount. The sun naturally triggers the correct hormone levels to help us fall asleep when we're supposed to and wake up when we're supposed to.

That's why it is important to get good sun exposure, among other benefits as well.

Obviously, you cannot get adequate sun exposure every day because some days are overcast and others aren't. But, it's important to try to get sun when you can. Simply go for a walk during lunch and talk with your colleagues outside, for example.

87. MAKE A ROUTINE YOU CAN STICK WITH

If you want to be productive, stick to a routine.

Routines are incredibly effective tools when it comes to making sure you get done what you need to get done.

It ensures that you have a place in your day for each item that should get done. What's more, it reduces the chances of you forgetting to do each item.

And routines are not just for your PhD. For example, you can have regular meetings, certain periods for reading each day, certain times to check emails (tip #84), certain times for taking breaks (tip #99), and so on. But, you should also have routines for your outside life to make sure you do what is good for you. For example, making sure that each Thursday at 6:30 pm, you go to the gym. Or, every Friday, you have dinner with your friends. Or, every Sunday afternoon, you do whatever you like – go bowling or knit something, whatever you like.

One highly effective way of enforcing a routine is by putting your daily, and weekly, tasks into your phone's calendar. Set each task to give you a reminder when you need it. That way, it takes much of the thinking out of the equation and you can concentrate on what you're doing, while knowing that you won't miss anything.

One demographic that has difficulty with routines is parents. Understandably, young children are on their own schedules and trying to have a routine that fits theirs is difficult. In this case, organize with your partner, parents, or close and trusted friends, that at a certain time of the week, they take care of your children while you do the important tasks that you can't do while keeping an eye on them. And reciprocate with them so they can do the same some time during the week.

Routines help you keep a balanced life. Make sure to use them.

88. DO THINGS OUTSIDE OF ACADEMIA

One of the easiest things to do when doing your PhD is get sucked into academia 100%. Your entire life becomes academia-centric.

That is not good because we are so much more than just academia.

The easiest way to extricate part of our lives from academia is to do things outside of academia.

This ties into tips #20 and #51, where you need to ensure that you do things outside of academia.

If you have hobbies, make sure to keep them up. What's more, a PhD is actually a great chance to pick up new hobbies because you'll meet many different people during it and learn about their hobbies.

Doing things outside of academia is a great way to manage your mental health because you take a break from your work (tips #24 and #51).

89. MANAGE YOUR EMOTIONAL TIREDNESS

We often hear people talk about how tired they are, and we often talk about it too.

But, there are different types of tiredness. We can be physically tired and even emotionally tired.

Emotional tiredness is far more taxing because it is harder to gage and often ignored completely.

When you're emotionally tired, your productivity drops, along with your enthusiasm for life. For example, being emotionally tired results in needing more sleep, lacking physical energy to do anything, being cranky, and even depressed.

Emotional tiredness comes from being hammered with tasks and stressing all of the time. A PhD is a great environment for becoming emotionally tired simply because of how long it is.

How can you gage your emotional tiredness?

One easy way is to look at the physical signs – if you're lacking energy then it's likely due to being emotionally drained. If you don't feel as happy as you once did, then that's also another strong sign.

We will cover in the next couple of tips how to diffuse the emotional strain, but one additional way is to get some perspective; we all lose perspective when something becomes such a large part of our lives (tip #88). In fact, just because we focus on it so much, it naturally becomes far more important to us than it should be. For example, imagine if you failed your PhD? It would seem like the end of the world, right? I agree because I used to feel the exact same way – there was nothing worse.

However, I felt like that because I lacked perspective – I got caught up in my PhD and forgot that there was an outside world (tip #88).

In reality, if I failed, then that would be several years of hard work down the drain, but, I still would have gotten a lot out of those years – you learn and develop greatly.

What's more, that development and those additional skills help you in whatever other career you choose.

At most, failing your PhD is just a redirection, not even a setback. You might see it as a setback now, but in 20 years' time, it will be obvious that the path it sent you down was what suited you better. It's hard to realize that when you lose perspective of the fact that a PhD isn't everything – there are billions of people who don't have one and they're doing just fine. Not getting a PhD is not the end of the world.

90. SET DAILY GOALS FOR YOURSELF

Through this book, we have talked many times about losing motivation and staying motivated (for example, tips #5, #19, and #26).

One of the most effective ways to keep up motivation is to set daily goals for yourself.

This not only ensures that you work on the things that deserve to be worked on (tip #27), but when you achieve these daily goals, you feel proud of yourself.

Every time you achieve something, you get a little more belief in yourself. It's important to take advantage of this process during your PhD because if you only have the one ultimate goal of getting your PhD, then you'll have to go several years without ever getting a little win (tip #58).

The motivation you get every day by having daily tasks dramatically increases.

This leads to a virtuous cycle where every day that you set daily goals, you focus on what should be focused on today AND you get little hits of self-belief every time you complete one.

You may be reluctant to set daily goals for yourself out of fear of not meeting them. That's fine. Instead, break the goals down further (tip #18). It can be something as simple as, "I want to get one idea down on paper today". One idea is easy to do. What's more, did you notice how the goal is, "get one IDEA down" and not, "write one SENTENCE"?

The reason why is because PhD students, and researchers in general, love to think. We love to come up with ideas. Many hate writing. For many, getting one idea down on paper is far easier to do than to write aimlessly one sentence.

If I have an idea, I can write pages on it happily. If I don't have an idea, then writing even one sentence is excruciating. What's more, writing one sentence without having the idea behind it is a waste of time, even if you're trying to boost your communication skills (tip #33) because communication is about conveying an idea. If you don't have an idea, then you have nothing to convey. So, if you are struggling to write the amount of words you want, change from saying, "I want to write this many words", to, "I want to write this idea down". It will help.

Another reason why PhD students, and people in general, don't like setting daily goals is because it seems like a waste of time. That 20 minutes you spend in the morning should be used to do real work.

This belief cannot be more mistaken. If you do not know what you should do, then no amount of work can get you there.

A little bit of intelligence overcomes A LOT of force. So, using 20 minutes in the morning to plan your goals (or even setting those goals the day before), is THE most efficient and effective use of your time.

91. MAKE A LIST OF ALL THE REASONS WHY YOU WANT A PHD

Another technique for keeping up motivation is to make a list of all the things you want your PhD for.

The logic behind this is simple – the more reasons you have, the more motivation you have to complete it.

For example, if my list of reasons consists solely of, "I want the Doctor title", then that's fine, but it's just one reason.

Instead, if your list consisted of the following reasons,

- To have the Doctor title
- To get into research
- To become a professor
- To be more respected
- To solve a problem I am passionate about

Then, these five reasons will keep you going longer than just the one sole reason.

So, make a list of every reason why you want to get a PhD. Add everything you can to it. The longer the list of reasons, the more effective it will be.

Then, get that list and put it somewhere you will see it regularly. You need to remind yourself of these reasons on a weekly, and even daily basis.

92. MEDITATE

This is a polarizing idea. Some people absolutely love it, others think it is some kind of "New-Age woo woo". By the end of this tip, I hope to have convinced you in a logical fashion how meditating regularly will help your PhD.

The idea of meditating is poorly understood. When most people think about it, they think of candles and incense. But that's just one form of meditation.

Meditation, at its core, is simply focusing solely on one thing.

With this more complete definition, it becomes obvious that meditation can take on all sorts of forms. When you stare out of the window blankly, that's meditation. When you go for a run, that's meditation. When you're focusing on cooking something you've never cooked before, that's meditation.

Anything that makes you focus solely on what you are doing is meditation – your mind has now become hyper-focused.

Do you think that the ability to focus solely on any given task in your PhD would be beneficial? For example, would you find it beneficial to be able to read a paper without thinking about your phone every few seconds? Or whether someone has gotten back to you about an email?

Would being able to focus solely on a task make it easier to complete it? Would it also produce a better result?

The more you meditate, the better you become at focusing your mind on the task at hand. The more you can focus, the deeper your level of thought. The deeper your level of thought, the more clearly you can think.

Would clearer thought help your PhD?

Would clearer thought increase the chances of finding a solution to any problem you have?

"Yes" to all of these questions.

I hope from this short logical train of thought, you are now convinced that meditation will greatly help your PhD.

To meditate, simply select anything you enjoy doing and focus on that. The harder and/or more unfamiliar the task, the more meditative it becomes because more and more mental energy is pulled away from everything else you were focusing on and directed to this task.

93. DAYDREAM

Akin to meditating is daydreaming.

Daydreaming is a great way of de-stressing, but also for getting good ideas.

Our thought patterns are based on our experiences. If we have experienced a certain outcome when we do a particular thing, then we expect that that outcome will be the same the next time.

This is good to some extent, however, it can limit our thoughts.

This is because much of the time, our experience is based on chance.

For example, say I need to interview some people, but some of them don't want to talk to me. This could be for all kinds of reasons. If, in the past, I have tried to appeal to these people but they refused, then I would build the expectation that appealing to those who have already declined is a waste of time.

However, there are so many potential reasons why these original people declined and refused any appeal. Most of these reasons, you are not privy to.

What's more, perhaps there are alternative ways of appealing to people that you haven't even thought of.

Daydreaming and letting your mind wander is a good way of

breaking through preconceived notions.

For example, with that last example, perhaps some of the people don't want to talk with you alone, or maybe they only want to talk with you alone and your original group-interviewing format doesn't work for them. Daydreaming a little helps you overcome any barriers you put up to begin with.

94. BE GRATEFUL FOR WHAT YOU HAVE ACHIEVED

Gratitude is one of the best ways to ensure motivation and happiness.

Yes, not everything in your PhD, and life, is perfect, but that doesn't mean that what you have achieved already is any less valuable.

What's more, by being grateful for what you've achieved already, you are inherently acknowledging that you can achieve and that instils belief in you – when things are bad, you still have the belief that you can get out of it and that makes you try harder simply because you're more motivated. You have done it before, and the very act of being grateful for your achievements inherently acknowledges this.

Be grateful for your achievements.

95. MAKE SURE TO STAY SOCIAL

One of the most common situations PhD students find themselves in is becoming more and more antisocial. It is a fairly normal progression because most PhD students, and researchers in general, get sucked into their research so much that they forget about the outside world (tips #76 and #88).

The general positive effect of interacting with other people cannot be overstated. We humans are very social creatures, even if many of us identify as introverts. Regardless of whether we're introverts or extroverts, almost all of us find the company of others familiar to us comforting.

If you don't remain social, then you will be cutting off something that makes you happier. This makes continuing your PhD harder.

What's more, staying social keeps your social skills sharp and these skills are not only highly valuable when it comes to communication (tips #31, #32, and #40), but also for networking (tip #41) and getting a job.

When you make your plan for the day, and even for the week, make sure to schedule time in for being social. It could even be one of your goals for the day (tip #90).

96. START LOOKING FOR YOUR NEXT JOB EARLY

One of the most frequently asked questions by PhD students is, "When should I start looking for a job?"

The answer to this is not what you'd expect. The answer is as soon as possible. The reason why is that "looking for a job" is not just about looking at ads placed online and applying for them, it's also about leveraging your network.

It's far easier to get a job through your network than through cold applications.

So, the very minute you start networking (tip #41) is when you're starting to look for a job.

Now, to answer the question in the manner that most PhD students intended the question; you should start actually applying for jobs about 9 months before you plan to finish. This time could be a little more or a little less, but 9 months is a good amount of time because it often takes employers some time to go through all of the candidates, interview them, make their decision, then organize for the chosen candidate to start working.

If you start applying over one year before you plan on finishing, then that's probably going to be a little too far out. However, there are some grants that need that much time – it's just that those grants are few and far between. What's more, if you start applying only 3 months before you finish, then there's little chance of getting a job before you finish, which means that you're going to have a gap between finishing and employment. That is not necessarily a bad thing – many PhD students would benefit from taking some time off. Some PhD students even just get part time jobs for a few months just to pay the bills and do something that isn't mentally demanding.

If you want to finish your PhD and move seamlessly into a job, then start applying about 9 months before you finish.

And this is another reminder to network! Start networking early!

97. KEEP AN UP-TO-DATE CV

When applying for a PhD position, you probably needed a CV of some sort. Once you get your position, it is also likely that you'll probably just forget about your CV.

You should keep your CV up-to-date throughout your PhD for a few reasons.

The first is that it makes it much easier to start applying for jobs (tip #97) – you already have your "master CV" ready and just need to extract the relevant information.

The second reason is that a PhD is long, and we do so many noteworthy things throughout it that we forget about 90% of them. By writing them into your master CV now, you have a record that you can refer to when customizing each CV for each position later in the future. If you don't record them now, then chances are that you'll forget about them later.

The third reason is that your CV is kind of like your professional achievement record. Each time you add something to it, there is hard evidence that you achieved something. That has a very powerful effect on our minds and we immediately feel more confident in ourselves. What's more, each time we go back to add something else to our CVs, we will naturally read through other things and that will remind us of just how much we've achieved.

Every couple of months, revisit your CV and update it.

98. BACKUP YOUR WORK REGULARLY

We all know that we should backup our work regularly because the risk of losing it is devastating for a PhD student – you can't get it back and that work was years in the making.

But, there are a few things to keep in mind when backing up your work.

The first is to make a time every week (or even more frequently if you have certain data that's very important) to do it. Put it in your calendar, add it to your phone's reminders, anything and everything that makes sure that you'll remember and DO IT!

The second thing to keep in mind is to back it up to a different device. A common mistake when backing up work is that the person just makes a copy of it and puts it on the same computer (more specifically, the same hard drive) that s/he is working on. While the effort is commendable, this does not remove all of the risk – a backup is there not only in the event that you accidentally delete something but also if something happens to your computer. It might break or be stolen, or just malfunction.

By backing up your work on a different device, this mitigates this risk.

The third thing to keep in mind is how to backup your work. The easiest way is just to copy and paste your entire hard drive to another hard drive (or on the cloud). This is fine, however, over time, you will have dozens of copies and if you want to find a certain item, it can become difficult to remember which version was the one you're after. If you do backup your work with this approach, then keep notes about what major differences there are between each version. Alternatively, you could just keep the latest copies of each file, if that is appropriate for your work.

So, backup your work regularly. Do it!

99. TAKE REGULAR BREAKS

We have mentioned in other tips (for example, tip #24) that breaks are good.

But, as we approach the end of this book, it's important to not only state it, but state it explicitly. It's one of the most important tips in this book.

Make sure to schedule breaks into your day. What's more, you don't have to wait for one of these scheduled breaks to take a break. Sometimes, we just feel out of energy, inspiration, motivation, etc.

Nothing in your PhD research is hard when you've got that inspiration and motivation to do it! It's getting to that inspiration and motivation that's the hard part.

Breaks are great for keeping these things up.

Take breaks, and often.

100. ENJOY THE JOURNEY!

Something that is often forgotten with all of the tasks and deadlines floating around is to enjoy the journey.

There was once a time in your life when you would have been thrilled to be where you are. Remember that time and make sure to enjoy what you're doing now because this will be the only time you do it.

Additionally, this will be one of the few times in your life where you can research almost anything you like and focus on learning. It's a unique opportunity.

Remember to enjoy it.

CONCLUSION

That is the end of these 100 tips for PhD students.

100 tips are A LOT of tips and you cannot expect to read them just once and implement them all immediately. You probably won't even be able to implement 50 of them in one try.

That's why we summed them all up below and you can go through them and recap.

Pick out the ones that you want to implement immediately – build them into your routine (tip #87) and then once you've done that, move onto the next ones in the list. Repeat this process until you're killing it!

We know you can.

SUMMARY OF THESE 100 TIPS

1. Be Yourself, And Not Someone Else

2. Pick A Good Supervisor

3. Keep Regular Contact With Your Supervisors

4. Be Honest With Yourself And Your Supervisors

5. Love Your PhD Topic

6. Have The Right Expectations, Not Necessarily "Realistic"

7. Formulate The "Question" Of Your PhD Simply

8. When First Starting, See Your Librarians

9. Take Advantage Of Resources Available At Your Library

10. Make A Plan Of Your PhD

11. Keep An Up-To-Date Plan Of Your Work

12. Work Smarter, Not Harder

13. Find And Apply For Research Grants And Scholarships

14. Read Up On Everything You Can About Your Topic Before You Start Your Dissertation

15. Make Notes Of Each Paper You've Read In A Simple Spreadsheet

16. Don't Be Intimidated By The Process of Going To Graduate School

17. Don't Worry About Getting Everything Done

18. If A Project Seems Like Too Much Work, Break It Down Into Smaller Steps

19. Work On At Least Two Things And Alternate Between Them

20. Don't Forget About Yourself As Well!

21. Set Aside Time Every Day To Reflect

22. Do The Work, But Don't Stress Over It

23. Don't Worry About Your Dissertation

24. It's Okay To Be A Little Lazy Sometimes!

25. Work In Short Bursts

26. Set Time Limits For Yourself

27. Manage Your Time Effectively

28. Be Flexible

29. Invest In Some Good Stationary Supplies, Like Pencils And Pens

30. Teach Your Subject!

31. Get Teaching Experience

32. Join Public Speaking Classes, Like Toastmasters

33. Write Every Day

34. Don't Be Afraid To Ask For Help When You Need It!

35. You'll Get Used To Dealing With Stress

36. Join A Union

37. Be Kind To Yourself

38. Make Friends!

39. Attend Conferences And Talks

40. Try To Attend A Conference Every Year

41. Network!

42. Look For Collaborations

43. Organize Your Paper's Author Order Early

44. Present "Negative" Findings

45. Wear Comfortable Clothes

46. Make Your Working Environment Comfortable

47. Use The "Nightshift" Function On Your Devices

48. Eat Well

49. Don't Forget To Have Fun!

50. Find An Exercise Routine That Works For You

51. Set Aside Time Each Day For Relaxation

52. Get Enough Sleep

53. Try Not To Compare Yourself With Others

54. Don't Lose Sight Of What You're Here For

55. Remember That You're Not Alone

56. Don't Get Discouraged By The Long Road Ahead Of You

57. Find A Way To Laugh Every Day!

58. Celebrate Every Little Win

59. Accept That You Did Your Best

60. Learn From Your Mistakes

61. Learn From The Mistakes Of Others

62. Don't Be Afraid To Admit That You're Wrong, Even To Yourself

63. When A Mistake Or Problem Is Discovered, Accept It And Don't Try To Hide It

64. Conduct Your Research Thoroughly

65. Get Your Friends And Colleagues To Help You Spot Potential Problems In Your Research

66. Commit To Your Plan

67. Learn How To Deal With Rejection

68. Be Open To Constructive Feedback

69. Be Open To Change

70. It's Okay If Things Aren't Going Exactly How You Want Them To Go

71. Make Sure You Keep Up With Your Reading

72. Go To Class Often

73. Take Notes In Class And Review Them Later

74. Ask Questions In Class, Even If They Seem Stupid Or Pointless

75. Don't Be Afraid To Talk To People

76. Find Someone You Can Trust And Lean On Them When You Need Help (Or Just Need A Friend)

77. You Can Never Know Too Much About Your Field

78. Don't Forget That This Is A Marathon, Not A Sprint

79. Understand Your Body-Clock And Abide By It

80. You Won't Like Your Supervisor All The Time, And That's Okay

81. Spend As Much Time As You Can Around Positive People And As Little Time As Possible Around Negative People

82. Give Other People Compliments On Their Work

83. Don't Leave Things To The Last Minute

84. Set Barriers For Yourself And Your Work

85. Remember That You Aren't The Only One Who Feels This Way, Everyone Does

86. Get Proper Sunlight Exposure Every Day

87. Make A Routine You Can Stick With

88. Do Things Outside Of Academia

89. Manage Your Emotional Tiredness

90. Set Daily Goals For Yourself

91. Make A List Of All The Reasons Why You Want A PhD

92. Meditate

93. Daydream

94. Be Grateful For What You Have Achieved

95. Make Sure To Stay Social

96. Start Looking For Your Next Job Early

97. Keep An Up-To-Date CV

98. Backup Your Work Regularly

99. Take Regular Breaks

100. Enjoy The Journey!

PHD VOICE NEW BOOK NOTIFICATIONS

We have had many PhD students ask us to keep writing new books on other PhD topics. So, we will do so.

If you would like to be notified when we publish a new book, please let us know here: https://phdvoice.org/phd-voice-new-book-notification/ or you can email us at: contact@phdvoice.org to let us know.

We will be happy to notify you. :)

Thank you and all the best with your PhD and career!

RESOURCES MENTIONED IN THIS BOOK

Blog post on how to pick a supervisor: https://phdvoice.org/how-to-pick-a-phd-supervisor/

7-minute YouTube video showing how to make a Gantt Chart in Excel: https://www.youtube.com/watch?v=ByimCyYnl2Y.

Spreadsheet for making notes about paper: https://phdvoice.org/free-resources/

How To Write An Academic Paper 101 book: https://phdvoice.org/product/writing-an-academic-paper-101/

Message from the Toastmasters' President: https://www.toastmasters.org/leadership-central/message-from-the-international-president

RATING THIS BOOK

Can we ask you a favor, please? Would you be able to rate this book on whichever platform you purchased it on?

It greatly helps us so we can continue to write more about other topics to help you further.

It also helps other PhD students know that this book contains useful information for them.

Thank you very much!

OTHER BOOKS
BY PHD VOICE

How To Write An Academic Paper 101

https://phdvoice.org/product/writing-an-academic-paper-101/

https://www.amazon.com/dp/1695576020

Supervising PhD Students, Effectively

https://phdvoice.org/product/supervising-phd-students/

https://www.amazon.com/dp/B0B4HJ2CFH

USEFUL SERVICES PHD VOICE OFFERS

High-Level Proofreading:

Would you like it to be easier to get your paper accepted?

Then, make sure to have it professionally proofread.

Writing an academic paper is great, but it's also important to have a skilled proofreader read your paper and correct any grammatical mistakes.

A paper with grammatical mistakes makes it harder to get it published. It can also confuse the reader, which reduces the number of citations you get. This impacts your career.

To help you get your paper published, and boost citations, we offer high-level academic proofreading.

We've proofread over 1,000 academic papers and dissertations, so we are highly skilled.

We also have many reviews from our clients, which you can find here: https://phdvoice.org/product/affordable-proofreading/.

If you need your paper proofread, let us know here: https://phdvoice.org/product/affordable-proofreading/!

Printed in Great Britain
by Amazon

26471692R00106